Tower Air Fryer
Cookbook for Beginners

1001 Super-Easy, Yummy & Tasty Recipes, Incl. Side Dishes, Desserts, Snacks and more

Clyde Hartz

CONTENTS

VEGETARIAN & VEGAN RECIPES... 67

SIDE DISHES RECIPES 78

DESSERTS RECIPES 88

APPENDIX : RECIPES INDEX 99

HOW TO USE YOUR AIR FRYER

THE BASICS

Air fryers work by rapid air cooking—evenly circulating hot air to cook fresh or frozen foods, which gives them the same crunchy bite and moist interiors produced by conventional deep fryers, all while never submerging them in cooking oils or fats. In other words, the air is the oil!

I love air frying so much that I've developed my own Todd English air fryer. But you can use this book with any basket air fryer.

PARTS OF THE AIR FRYER

Inside the air fryer unit is a removable heating chamber and a cooking basket. To take the cooking basket out of the heating chamber, just press the release button and lift it out.

Many air fryers also come with a removable rack, used for keeping meats off the bottom of the basket, or for steaming items with a little liquid underneath. If you're lucky, you have the Todd English Air Fryer, which also has a pizza pan that can be used for cooking pizza (naturally) and as a baking tin. If you don't have a pizza pan especially for your air fryer, you can use a glass, silicone, or metal oven-safe dish instead. No matter which you use, place it in the basket before cooking. (In order for the air fryer to operate, the heating chamber—with the cooking basket in it—must be secured in the air fryer.)

GETTING STARTED

To cook items in your air fryer, it's really as easy as throwing them in the basket and selecting the time and temperature! Some air fryers have presets (for instance, on my air fryer, you can select "Bacon," and it will automatically cook for 15 minutes at 370º F). But if your air fryer doesn't, or you're cooking something there isn't a preset for, I've included a handy chart here of common foods and their cook times and temps. Spraying a little nonstick cooking spray on the items first is usually a good idea, as it will help them crisp up. When cooking items that you want crunchy on all sides, it's also usually a good idea to pull out the basket halfway and flip the items, or simply shake the basket to toss them around a bit.

PREHEATING

It only takes about 3 minutes for an air fryer to preheat. In fact, if you want, you can simply add 3 minutes to the cook time and throw everything in without preheating. I told you it was easy!

AIR FRYER SAFETY TIPS

Air fryers are powerful machines, so make sure you stay safe.

• Air fryers get HOT! Especially if you've added oil or steaming liquid to the pan. While your food cooks, liquids will accumulate in the cooking chamber, so always use caution when removing the basket. After the cooking cycle is complete, the basket will be very hot! So after removing it, don't put it down anywhere that can't handle heat—it can burn your counter.

• Before cooking anything, make sure all the ingredients are inside the air fryer basket, to prevent any contact with the heating element.

• During the cooking cycle, hot air/steam is released through the air outlets. So keep your hands and face away from them, and don't place anything on top of the appliance during operation or otherwise cover the air inlets or outlets.

Be safe! Don't use the appliance if there is any damage to the plug, electrical cord, or any other parts. Don't use the air fryer (or plug it in) with wet hands, and don't leave it unattended while it's in operation. Unplug the fryer after you're done using it.

TAKING CARE OF YOUR AIR FRYER

WHERE TO KEEP YOUR AIR FRYER

I like to keep my air fryer handy on the kitchen counter, but wherever you end up using yours, make sure it's a flat, even, and stable surface. Make sure to leave at least 5 inches of free space around the back, sides, and top of the appliance for a clear air flow.

CLEANING YOUR AIR FRYER

Always wait 30 minutes for the air fryer to cool down before handling or cleaning it. You should clean the air fryer after

every use by wiping down the outside with a moist cloth; cleaning the heating chamber and cooking basket by hand with soap and water in the kitchen sink; and cleaning the inside of the appliance with a damp (wrung-out), non-abrasive sponge, wiping away any food debris and grease. Never clean any part of an air fryer with metal kitchen utensils or abrasive cleaning materials because they can damage the nonstick coating. If there's debris stuck to the basket or bottom of the pan, simply soak it in hot, soapy water for about 10 minutes to loosen it up before cleaning. If necessary, you can clean the heating element with a wet cleaning brush to remove debris (again, just make sure it's completely cool first!).

AIR FRYER COOKING TIPS

Air fryers are really easy to use, but here are some tips for making sure you get the most out of them!

• Any food that can be cooked in a microwave or oven can be cooked in an air fryer.

• To give food a crispy texture, spray cooking oil or nonstick spray over the ingredients before adding them to the basket. Alternatively, you can add a small amount (3–4 tablespoons) of oil to the pan before cooking. (Never overfill, as this will damage the air fryer.)

• Smaller ingredients usually require a slightly shorter cooking time than larger ingredients. Shaking smaller ingredients halfway during the cooking time ensures they'll be evenly cooked.

• To steam food, add a small amount (3–4 table-spoons) of liquid, such as water or broth, to the pan after adding the ingredients. (Never overfill, as this will damage the air fryer.)

• You can also use an air fryer to reheat food by setting the temperature to 300° F for up to 10 minutes.

• See the Quick-Reference Cooking Chart for a cheat sheet on how long to cook most foods.

Measurement Conversions

BASIC KITCHEN CONVERSIONS & EQUIVALENTS

DRY MEASUREMENTS CONVERSION CHART

3 TEASPOONS = 1 TABLESPOON = 1/16 CUP

6 TEASPOONS = 2 TABLESPOONS = 1/8 CUP

12 TEASPOONS = 4 TABLESPOONS = 1/4 CUP

24 TEASPOONS = 8 TABLESPOONS = 1/2 CUP

36 TEASPOONS = 12 TABLESPOONS = 3/4 CUP

48 TEASPOONS = 16 TABLESPOONS = 1 CUP

METRIC TO US COOKING CONVERSIONS

OVEN TEMPERATURES

120 °C = 250 °F

160 °C = 320 °F

180° C = 350 °F

205 °C = 400 °F

220 °C = 425 °F

LIQUID MEASUREMENTS CONVERSION CHART

8 FLUID OUNCES = 1 CUP = 1/2 PINT = 1/4 QUART

16 FLUID OUNCES = 2 CUPS = 1 PINT = 1/2 QUART

32 FLUID OUNCES = 4 CUPS = 2 PINTS = 1 QUART

= 1/4 GALLON

128 FLUID OUNCES = 16 CUPS = 8 PINTS = 4 QUARTS = 1 GALLON

BAKING IN GRAMS

1 CUP FLOUR = 140 GRAMS

1 CUP SUGAR = 150 GRAMS

1 CUP POWDERED SUGAR = 160 GRAMS

1 CUP HEAVY CREAM = 235 GRAMS

VOLUME

1 MILLILITER = 1/5 TEASPOON

5 ML = 1 TEASPOON

15 ML = 1 TABLESPOON

240 ML = 1 CUP OR 8 FLUID OUNCES

1 LITER = 34 FL. OUNCES

WEIGHT

1 GRAM = .035 OUNCES

100 GRAMS = 3.5 OUNCES

500 GRAMS = 1.1 POUNDS

1 KILOGRAM = 35 OUNCES

US TO METRIC COOKING CONVERSIONS

1/5 TSP = 1 ML

1 TSP = 5 ML

1 TBSP = 15 ML

1 FL OUNCE = 30 ML

1 CUP = 237 ML

1 PINT (2 CUPS) = 473 ML

1 QUART (4 CUPS) = .95 LITER

1 GALLON (16 CUPS) = 3.8 LITERS

1 OZ = 28 GRAMS

1 POUND = 454 GRAMS

BUTTER

1 CUP BUTTER = 2 STICKS = 8 OUNCES = 230 GRAMS = 8 TABLESPOONS

WHAT DOES 1 CUP EQUAL

1 CUP = 8 FLUID OUNCES

1 CUP = 16 TABLESPOONS

1 CUP = 48 TEASPOONS

1 CUP = 1/2 PINT

1 CUP = 1/4 QUART

1 CUP = 1/16 GALLON

1 CUP = 240 ML

BAKING PAN CONVERSIONS

1 CUP ALL-PURPOSE FLOUR = 4.5 OZ

1 CUP ROLLED OATS = 3 OZ 1 LARGE EGG = 1.7 OZ

1 CUP BUTTER = 8 OZ 1 CUP MILK = 8 OZ

1 CUP HEAVY CREAM = 8.4 OZ

1 CUP GRANULATED SUGAR = 7.1 OZ

1 CUP PACKED BROWN SUGAR = 7.75 OZ

1 CUP VEGETABLE OIL = 7.7 OZ

1 CUP UNSIFTED POWDERED SUGAR = 4.4 OZ

BAKING PAN CONVERSIONS

9-INCH ROUND CAKE PAN = 12 CUPS

10-INCH TUBE PAN =16 CUPS

11-INCH BUNDT PAN = 12 CUPS

9-INCH SPRINGFORM PAN = 10 CUPS

9 X 5 INCH LOAF PAN = 8 CUPS

9-INCH SQUARE PAN = 8 CUPS

Sauces & Snack And Appetiser Recipes

Sweet Potato Crisps

Servings: 4

Ingredients:

- 1 sweet potato, peeled and thinly sliced
- 2 tbsp oil
- ¼ tsp salt
- ¼ tsp pepper
- 1 tsp chopped rosemary
- Cooking spray

Directions:

1. Place all ingredients in a bowl and mix well
2. Place in the air fryer and cook at 175°C for about 15 minutes until crispy

Stuffed Mushrooms

Servings: 24

Ingredients:

- 24 mushrooms
- ½ pepper, sliced
- ½ diced onion
- 1 small carrot, diced
- 200g grated cheese
- 2 slices bacon, diced
- 100g sour cream

Directions:

1. Place the mushroom stems, pepper, onion, carrot and bacon in a pan and cook for about 5 minutes
2. Stir in cheese and sour cream, cook until well combined
3. Heat the air fryer to 175°C
4. Add stuffing to each of the mushrooms
5. Place in the air fryer and cook for 8 minutes

Mini Calzones

Servings: 16

Ingredients:

- Flour for rolling out the dough
- 1 round pizza dough
- 100g pizza sauce

Directions:

1. Roll out the dough to ¼ inch thick
2. Cut out 8-10 dough rounds using a cutter
3. Re-roll the dough and cut out another 6 rounds
4. Top each round with pizza sauce, cheese and pepperoni
5. Fold dough over and pinch the edges to seal
6. Heat the air fryer to 190°C
7. Place the calzone in the air fryer and cook for about 8 minutes until golden brown

Italian Rice Balls

Servings: 2

Ingredients:

- 400g cooked rice
- 25g breadcrumbs, plus an extra 200g for breading
- 2 tbsp flour, plus an extra 2 tbsp for breading
- 1 tbsp cornstarch, plus an extra 3 tbsp for breading
- 1 chopped bell pepper
- 1 chopped onion
- 2 tbsp olive oil
- 1 tsp red chilli flakes
- 5 chopped mozzarella cheese sticks
- A little water for the breading
- Salt and pepper for seasoning

Directions:

1. Place the cooked rice into a bowl and mash with a fork. Place to one side
2. Take a saucepan and add the oil, salting the onion and peppers until they're both soft
3. Add the chilli flakes and a little salt and combine
4. Add the mixture to the mashed rice and combine
5. Add the 2 tbsp flour and 1 tbsp cornstarch, along with the 25g breadcrumbs and combine well
6. Use your hands to create balls with the mixture
7. Stuff a piece of the mozzarella inside the balls and form around it
8. Take a bowl and add the rest of the flour, corn starch and a little seasoning, with a small amount of water to create a thick batter
9. Take another bowl and add the rest of the breadcrumbs
10. Dip each rice ball into the batter and then the breadcrumbs
11. Preheat the air fryer to 220°C
12. Cook for 6 minutes, before shaking and cooking for another 6 minutes

Potato Patties

Servings: 12

Ingredients:

- 150g instant mash
- 50g peas and carrots
- 2 tbsp coriander
- 1 tbsp oil
- 100ml hot water
- ½ tsp turmeric
- ½ tsp cayenne
- ½ tsp salt
- ½ tsp cumin seeds
- ¼ tsp ground cumin

Directions:

1. Place all the ingredients in a bowl. Mix well cover and stand for 10 minutes
2. Preheat the air fryer to 200°C
3. Spray the air fryer with cooking spray
4. Make 12 patties, place in the air fryer and cook for 10 minutes

Pretzel Bites

Servings: 2

Ingredients:

- 650g flour
- 2.5 tsp active dry yeast
- 260ml hot water
- 1 tsp salt
- 4 tbsp melted butter
- 2 tbsp sugar

Directions:

1. Take a large bowl and add the flour, sugar and salt
2. Take another bowl and combine the hot water and yeast, stirring until the yeast has dissolved
3. Then, add the yeast mixture to the flour mixture and use your hands to combine
4. Knead for 2 minutes
5. Cover the bowl with a kitchen towel for around half an hour
6. Divide the dough into 6 pieces
7. Preheat the air fryer to 260°C
8. Take each section of dough and tear off a piece, rolling it in your hands to create a rope shape, that is around 1" in thickness
9. Cut into 2" strips
10. Place the small dough balls into the air fryer and leave a little space in-between
11. Cook for 6 minutes
12. Once cooked, remove and brush with melted butter and sprinkle salt on top

Thai Bites

Servings: 4

Ingredients:

- 400g pork mince
- 1 onion
- 1 tsp garlic paste
- 1 tbsp soy
- 1 tbsp Worcester sauce
- Salt and pepper
- 2 tsp Thai curry paste
- ½ lime juice and zest
- 1 tsp mixed spice
- 1 tsp Chinese spice
- 1 tsp coriander

Directions:

1. Place all ingredients in a bowl and mix well
2. Shape into balls
3. Place in the air fryer and cook at 180ºC for 15 minutes

Mac & Cheese Bites

Servings: 14

Ingredients:

- 200g mac and cheese
- 2 eggs
- 200g panko breadcrumbs
- Cooking spray

Directions:

1. Place drops of mac and cheese on parchment paper and freeze for 1 hour
2. Beat the eggs in a bowl, add the breadcrumbs to another bowl
3. Dip the mac and cheese balls in the egg then into the breadcrumbs
4. Heat the air fryer to 190ºC
5. Place in the air fryer, spray with cooking spray and cook for 15 minutes

Jalapeño Poppers

Servings: 2

Ingredients:

- 10 jalapeños, halved and deseeded
- 100g cream cheese
- 50g parsley
- 150g breadcrumbs

Directions:

1. Mix 1/2 the breadcrumbs with the cream cheese
2. Add the parsley
3. Stuff the peppers with the cream cheese mix
4. Top the peppers with the remaining breadcrumbs
5. Heat the air fryer to 185°C
6. Place in the air fryer and cook for 6-8 minutes

Chicken & Bacon Parcels

Servings: 4

Ingredients:

- 2 chicken breasts, boneless and skinless
- 200ml BBQ sauce
- 7 slices of bacon, cut lengthwise into halves
- 2 tbsp brown sugar

Directions:

1. Preheat the air fryer to 220°C
2. Cut the chicken into strips, you should have 7 in total
3. Wrap two strips of the bacon around each piece of chicken
4. Brush the BBQ sauce over the top and sprinkle with the brown sugar
5. Place the chicken into the basket and cook for 5 minutes
6. Turn the chicken over and cook for another 5 minutes

Pasta Chips

Servings: 2

Ingredients:

- 300g dry pasta bows
- 1 tbsp olive oil
- 1 tbsp nutritional yeast
- 1½ tsp Italian seasoning
- ½ tsp salt

Directions:

1. Cook the pasta for half the time stated on the packet
2. Drain and mix with the oil, yeast, seasoning and salt
3. Place in the air fryer and cook at 200°C for 5 minutes shake and cook for a further 3 minutes until crunchy

Bacon Smokies

Servings: 8

Ingredients:
- 150g little smokies (pieces)
- 150g bacon
- 50g brown sugar
- Toothpicks

Directions:
1. Cut the bacon strips into thirds
2. Put the brown sugar into a bowl
3. Coat the bacon with the sugar
4. Wrap the bacon around the little smokies and secure with a toothpick
5. Heat the air fryer to 170ºC
6. Place in the air fryer and cook for 10 minutes until crispy

Asian Devilled Eggs

Servings: 12

Ingredients:
- 6 large eggs
- 2 tbsp mayo
- 1 ½ tsp sriracha
- 1 ½ tsp sesame oil
- 1 tsp soy sauce
- 1 tsp dijon mustard
- 1 tsp finely grated ginger
- 1 tsp rice vinegar
- 1 chopped green onion
- Toasted sesame seeds

Directions:
1. Set air fryer to 125ºC
2. Place eggs in the air fryer and cook for 15 minutes
3. Remove from the air fryer and place in a bowl of iced water for 10 minutes
4. Peel and cut in half
5. Scoop out the yolks and place in a food processor
6. Add the ingredients apart from the sesame seeds and green onion and combine until smooth
7. Place in a piping bag and pipe back into the egg whites
8. Garnish with seeds and green onion

Tortellini Bites

Servings: 6

Ingredients:

- 200g cheese tortellini
- 150g flour
- 100g panko bread crumbs
- 50g grated parmesan
- 1 tsp dried oregano
- 2 eggs
- ½ tsp garlic powder
- ½ tsp chilli flakes
- Salt
- Pepper

Directions:

1. Cook the tortellini according to the packet instructions
2. Mix the panko, parmesan, oregano, garlic powder, chilli flakes salt and pepper in a bowl
3. Beat the eggs in another bowl and place the flour in a third bowl
4. Coat the tortellini in flour, then egg and then in the panko mix
5. Place in the air fryer and cook at 185°C for 10 minutes until crispy
6. Serve with marinara sauce for dipping

Tostones

Servings: 4

Ingredients:

- 2 unripe plantains
- Olive oil cooking spray
- 300ml of water
- Salt to taste

Directions:

1. Preheat the air fryer to 200°C
2. Slice the tips off the plantain
3. Cut the plantain into 1 inch chunks
4. Place in the air fryer spray with oil and cook for 5 minutes
5. Remove the plantain from the air fryer and smash to ½ inch pieces
6. Soak in a bowl of salted water
7. Remove from the water and return to the air fryer season with salt cook for 5 minutes
8. Turn and cook for another 5 minutes

Spicy Peanuts

Servings: 8

Ingredients:

- 2 tbsp olive oil
- 3 tbsp seafood seasoning
- ½ tsp cayenne
- 300g raw peanuts
- Salt to taste

Directions:

1. Preheat the air fryer to 160°C
2. Whisk together ingredients in a bowl and stir in the peanuts
3. Add to air fryer and cook for 10 minutes, shake then cook for a further 10 minutes
4. Sprinkle with salt and cook for another 5 minutes

Korean Chicken Wings

Servings: 2

Ingredients:

- 25ml soy sauce
- 40g brown sugar
- 2 tbsp hot pepper paste
- 1 tsp sesame oil
- ½ tsp ginger paste
- ½ tsp garlic paste
- 2 green onions, chopped
- 400g chicken wings
- 1 tbsp vegetable oil

Directions:

1. Preheat air fryer to 200°C
2. Place all ingredients apart from chicken wings and vegetable oil in a pan and simmer for about 4 minutes set aside
3. Massage the vegetable oil into the chicken wings
4. Place in the air fryer and cook for about 10 minutes
5. Turn and cook for a further 10 minutes
6. Coat the wings in the sauce and return to the air fryer
7. Cook for about 2 minutes

Popcorn Tofu

Servings: 4

Ingredients:

- 400g firm tofu
- 100g chickpea flour
- 100g oatmeal
- 2 tbsp yeast
- 150ml milk
- 400g breadcrumbs
- 1 tsp garlic powder
- 1 tsp onion powder
- 1 tbsp dijon mustard
- ½ tsp salt
- ½ tsp pepper
- 2 tbsp vegetable bouillon

Directions:

1. Rip the tofu into pieces. Place the breadcrumbs into a bowl, in another bowl mix the remaining ingredients
2. Dip the tofu into the batter mix and then dip into the breadcrumbs
3. Heat the air fryer to 175°C
4. Place the tofu in the air fryer and cook for 12 minutes shaking halfway through

Beetroot Crisps

Servings: 2

Ingredients:

- 3 medium beetroots
- 2 tbsp oil
- Salt to taste

Directions:

1. Peel and thinly slice the beetroot
2. Coat with the oil and season with salt
3. Preheat the air fryer to 200°C
4. Place in the air fryer and cook for 12-18 minutes until crispy

Air-fried Pickles

Servings: 4

Ingredients:

- 1/2 cup mayonnaise
- 2 tsp sriracha sauce
- 1 jar dill pickle slices
- 1 egg
- 2 tbsp milk
- 50g flour
- 50g cornmeal
- ½ tsp seasoned salt
- ¼ tsp paprika
- ¼ tsp garlic powder
- ⅛ tsp pepper
- Cooking spray

Directions:

1. Mix the mayo and sriracha together in a bowl and set aside
2. Heat the air fryer to 200°C
3. Drain the pickles and pat dry
4. Mix egg and milk together, in another bowl mix all the remaining ingredients
5. Dip the pickles in the egg mix then in the flour mix
6. Spray the air fryer with cooking spray
7. Cook for about 4 minutes until crispy

Pork Jerky

Servings: 35

Ingredients:

- 300g mince pork
- 1 tbsp oil
- 1 tbsp sriracha
- 1 tbsp soy
- ½ tsp pink curing salt
- 1 tbsp rice vinegar
- ½ tsp salt
- ½ tsp pepper
- ½ tsp onion powder

Directions:

1. Mix all ingredients in a bowl until combined
2. Refrigerate for about 8 hours
3. Shape into sticks and place in the air fryer
4. Heat the air fryer to 160ºC
5. Cook for 1 hour turn then cook for another hour
6. Turn again and cook for another hour
7. Cover with paper and sit for 8 hours

Mini Aubergine Parmesan Pizza

Servings: 8

Ingredients:

- 1 aubergine, cut into ½ inch slices
- Salt to taste
- 1 egg
- 1 tbsp water
- 100g bread crumbs
- 75g grated parmesan
- 6 tbsp pizza sauce
- 50g sliced olives
- 75g grated mozzarella
- Basil to garnish

Directions:

1. Preheat air fryer to 160ºC
2. Mix egg and water together and in another bowl mix the breadcrumbs and parmesan
3. Dip the aubergine in the egg then coat with the breadcrumbs
4. Place in the air fryer and cook for 10 minutes
5. Spoon pizza sauce on the aubergine, add olives and sprinkle with mozzarella
6. Cook for about 4 minutes until cheese has melted

Breakfast & Snacks And Fries Recipes

Plantain Fries

Servings: 2

Ingredients:

- 1 ripe plantain (yellow and brown outside skin)
- 1 teaspoon olive oil
- ¼ teaspoon salt

Directions:

1. Preheat the air-fryer to 180°C/350°F.
2. Peel the plantain and slice into fries about 6 x 1 cm/2½ x ½ in. Toss the fries in oil and salt, making sure every fry is coated.
3. Tip into the preheated air-fryer in a single layer (you may need to cook them in two batches, depending on the size of your air-fryer) and air-fry for 13–14 minutes until brown on the outside and soft on the inside. Serve immediately.

Courgette Fries

Servings: 2

Ingredients:

- 1 courgette/zucchini
- 3 tablespoons plain/all-purpose flour (gluten-free if you wish)
- ¼ teaspoon salt
- ¼ teaspoon freshly ground black pepper
- 60 g/¾ cup dried breadcrumbs (gluten-free if you wish; see page 9)
- 1 teaspoon dried oregano
- 20 g/¼ cup finely grated Parmesan
- 1 egg, beaten

Directions:

1. Preheat the air-fryer to 180°C/350°F.
2. Slice the courgette/zucchini into fries about 1.5 x 1.5 x 5 cm/⅝ x ⅝ x 2 in.
3. Season the flour with salt and pepper. Combine the breadcrumbs with the oregano and Parmesan.
4. Dip the courgettes/zucchini in the flour (shaking off any excess flour), then the egg, then the seasoned breadcrumbs.
5. Add the fries to the preheated air-fryer and air-fry for 15 minutes. They should be crispy on the outside but soft on the inside. Serve immediately.

Egg & Bacon Breakfast Cups

Servings: 8

Ingredients:

- 6 eggs
- 1 chopped red pepper
- 1 chopped green pepper
- 1 chopped yellow pepper
- 2 tbsp double cream
- 50g chopped spinach
- 50g grated cheddar cheese
- 50g grated mozzarella cheese
- 3 slices of cooked bacon, crumbled into pieces

Directions:

1. Take a large mixing bowl and crack the eggs
2. Add the cream and season with a little salt and pepper, combining everything well
3. Add the peppers, spinach, onions, both cheeses, and the crumbled bacon, combining everything once more
4. You will need silicone moulds or cups for this part, and you should pour equal amounts of the mixture into 8 cups
5. Cook at 150ºC for around 12 or 15 minutes, until the eggs are cooked properly

Meaty Egg Cups

Servings: 4

Ingredients:

- 8 slices of toasted sandwich bread
- 2 slices of ham
- 4 eggs
- Salt and pepper to taste
- Butter for greasing

Directions:

1. Take 4 ramekins and grease the insides with a little butter
2. Flatten the slices of toast with a rolling pin and arrange inside the ramekins - two in each
3. Line the inside of each ramekin with a slice of ham
4. Crack one egg into each ramekin
5. Season with a little salt and pepper
6. Place the ramekins into the air fryer and cook at 160ºC for 15 minutes
7. Remove from the fryer and wait to cool just slightly
8. Remove and serve

Easy Cheesy Scrambled Eggs

Servings: 1

Ingredients:

- 1 tbsp butter
- 2 eggs
- 100g grated cheese
- 2 tbsp milk
- Salt and pepper for seasoning

Directions:

1. Add the butter inside the air fryer pan and cook at 220ºC until the butter has melted
2. Add the eggs and milk to a bowl and combine, seasoning to your liking
3. Pour the eggs into the butter panned cook for 3 minutes, stirring around lightly to scramble
4. Add the cheese and cook for another 2 more minutes

Morning Sausage Wraps

Servings: 8

Ingredients:

- 8 sausages, chopped into pieces
- 2 slices of cheddar cheese, cut into quarters
- 1 can of regular crescent roll dough
- 8 wooden skewers

Directions:

1. Take the dough and separate each one
2. Cut open the sausages evenly
3. The one of your crescent rolls and on the widest part, add a little sausage and then a little cheese
4. Roll the dough and tuck it until you form a triangle
5. Repeat this for four times and add into your air fryer
6. Cook at 190ºC for 3 minutes
7. Remove your dough and add a skewer for serving
8. Repeat with the other four pieces of dough

Potato Fries

Servings: 2

Ingredients:

- 2 large potatoes (baking potato size)
- 1 teaspoon olive oil
- salt

Directions:

1. Peel the potatoes and slice into fries about 5 x 1.5cm/¾ x ¾ in. by the length of the potato. Submerge the fries in a bowl of cold water and place in the fridge for about 10 minutes.
2. Meanwhile, preheat the air-fryer to 160ºC/325ºF.
3. Drain the fries thoroughly, then toss in the oil and season. Tip into the preheated air-fryer in a single layer (you may need to cook them in two batches, depending on the size of your air-fryer). Air-fry for 15 minutes, tossing once during cooking by shaking the air-fryer drawer, then increase the temperature of the air-fryer to 200ºC/400ºF and cook for a further 3 minutes. Serve immediately.

Potato & Chorizo Frittata

Servings: 2

Ingredients:

- 3 eggs
- 1 sliced chorizo sausage
- 1 potato, boiled and cubed
- 50g feta cheese
- 50g frozen sweetcorn
- A pinch of salt
- 1 tbsp olive oil

Directions:

1. Add a little olive oil to the frying basket
2. Add the corn, potato, and sliced chorizo to the basket
3. Cook at 180°C until the sausage is a little brown
4. In a small bowl, beat together the eggs with a little seasoning
5. Pour the eggs into the pan
6. Crumble the feta on top
7. Cook for 5 minutes
8. Remove and serve in slices

French Toast

Servings: 2

Ingredients:

- 2 beaten eggs
- 2 tbsp softened butter
- 4 slices of sandwich bread
- 1 tsp cinnamon
- 1 tsp nutmeg
- 1 tsp ground cloves
- 1 tsp maple syrup

Directions:

1. Preheat your fryer to 180°C
2. Take a bowl and add the eggs, salt, cinnamon, nutmeg, and cloves, combining well
3. Take your bread and butter each side, cutting into strips
4. Dip the bread slices into the egg mixture
5. Arrange each slice into the basket of your fryer
6. Cook for 2 minutes
7. Take the basket out and spray with a little cooking spray
8. Turn over the slices and place back into the fryer
9. Cook for 4 minutes
10. Remove and serve with maple syrup

Easy Air Fryer Sausage

Servings: 5

Ingredients:

- 5 uncooked sausages
- 1 tbsp mustard
- Salt and pepper for seasoning

Directions:

1. Line the basket of your fryer with parchment paper
2. Arrange the sausages inside the basket
3. Set to 180°C and cook for 15 minutes
4. Turn the sausages over and cook for another 5 minutes
5. Remove and cool
6. Drizzle the mustard over the top and season to your liking

Hard Boiled Eggs Air Fryer Style

Servings: 2

Ingredients:

- 4 large eggs
- 1 tsp cayenne pepper
- Salt and pepper for seasoning

Directions:

1. Preheat the air fryer to 220°C
2. Take a wire rack and place inside the air fryer
3. Lay the eggs on the rack
4. Cook for between 15-17 minutes, depending upon how you like your eggs
5. Remove from the fryer and place in a bowl of cold water for around 5 minutes
6. Peel and season with the cayenne and the salt and pepper

Oozing Baked Eggs

Servings: 2

Ingredients:

- 4 eggs
- 140g smoked gouda cheese, cut into small pieces
- Salt and pepper to taste

Directions:

1. You will need two ramekin dishes and spray each one before using
2. Crack two eggs into each ramekin dish
3. Add half of the Gouda cheese to each dish
4. Season and place into the air fryer
5. Cook at 350°C for 15 minutes, until the eggs are cooked as you like them

Blueberry Bread

Servings: 8

Ingredients:

- 260ml milk
- 3 eggs
- 25g protein powder
- 400g frozen blueberries
- 600g bisquick or pancake mixture

Directions:

1. Take a large mixing bowl and combine all ingredients until smooth
2. Preheat the air fryer to 250°C
3. Place the mixture into a loaf tin
4. Place the tin into the air fryer and cook for 30 minutes
5. A toothpick should come out clean if the bread is cooked

Toad In The Hole, Breakfast Style

Servings: 4

Ingredients:

- 1 sheet of puff pastry (defrosted)
- 4 eggs
- 4 tbsp grated cheese (cheddar works well)
- 4 slices of cooked ham, cut into pieces
- Chopped fresh herbs of your choice

Directions:

1. Preheat your air fryer to 200°C
2. Take your pastry sheet and place it on a flat surface, cutting it into four pieces
3. Take two of the pastry sheets and place them inside your fryer, cooking for up to 8 minutes, until done
4. Remove the pastry and flatten the centre down with a spoon, to form a deep hole
5. Add a tablespoon of the cheese and a tablespoon of the ham into the hole
6. Crack one egg into the hole
7. Return the pastry to the air fryer and cook for another 6 minutes, or until the egg is done as you like it
8. Remove and allow to cool
9. Repeat the process with the rest of the pastry remaining
10. Sprinkle fresh herbs on top and serve

Tangy Breakfast Hash

Servings: 6

Ingredients:

- 2 tbsp olive oil
- 2 sweet potatoes, cut into cubes
- 1 tbsp smoked paprika
- 1 tsp salt
- 1 tsp black pepper
- 2 slices of bacon, cut into small pieces

Directions:

1. Preheat your air fryer to 200°C
2. Pour the olive oil into a large mixing bowl
3. Add the bacon, seasonings, potatoes and toss to evenly coat
4. Transfer the mixture into the air fryer and cook for 12-16 minutes
5. Stir after 10 minutes and continue to stir periodically for another 5 minutes

Baba Ganoush

Servings: 4

Ingredients:

- 1 large aubergine/eggplant, sliced in half lengthways
- ½ teaspoon salt
- 5 tablespoons olive oil
- 1 bulb garlic
- 30 g/2 tablespoons tahini or nut butter
- 2 tablespoons freshly squeezed lemon juice
- ½ teaspoon ground cumin
- ¼ teaspoon smoked paprika
- salt and freshly ground black pepper
- 3 tablespoons freshly chopped flat-leaf parsley

Directions:

1. Preheat the air-fryer to 200°C/400°F.

2. Lay the aubergine/eggplant halves cut side up. Sprinkle over the salt, then drizzle over 1 tablespoon of oil. Cut the top off the garlic bulb, brush the exposed cloves with a little olive oil, then wrap in foil. Place the aubergine/eggplant and foil-wrapped garlic in the preheated air-fryer and air-fry for 15–20 minutes until the inside of the aubergine is soft and buttery in texture.

3. Scoop the flesh of the aubergine into a bowl. Squeeze out about 1 tablespoon of the cooked garlic and add to the bowl with the remaining 4 tablespoons of olive oil, the tahini/nut butter, lemon juice, spices and salt and pepper to taste. Mix well and serve with fresh flat-leaf parsley sprinkled over.

Monte Cristo Breakfast Sandwich

Servings: 4

Ingredients:

- 1 egg
- 2 slices of sandwich bread
- 1/4 tsp vanilla extract
- 4 slices of sliced Swiss cheese
- 4 slices of sliced deli ham
- 4 slices of sliced turkey
- 1 tsp melted butter
- Powdered sugar for serving

Directions:

1. In a small bowl, mix together the egg and vanilla extract, combining well
2. Take your bread and assemble your sandwich, starting with a slice of cheese, then the ham, turkey, and then another slice of the cheese, with the other slice of bread on the top
3. Compress the sandwich a little, so it cooks better
4. Take a piece of cooking foil and brush over it with the butter
5. Take your sandwich and dip each side into the egg mixture, leaving it to one side for around half a minute
6. Place the sandwich on the foil and place it inside your fryer
7. Cook at 200ºC for around 10 minutes, before turning the sandwich over and cooking for another 8 minutes
8. Transfer your sandwich onto a plate and sprinkle with a little powdered sugar

Easy Omelette

Servings: 1

Ingredients:

- 50ml milk
- 2 eggs
- 60g grated cheese, any you like
- Any garnishes you like, such as mushrooms, peppers, etc.

Directions:

1. Take a small mixing bowl and crack the eggs inside, whisking with the milk
2. Add the salt and garnishes and combine again
3. Grease a 6x3" pan and pour the mixture inside
4. Arrange the pan inside the air fryer basket
5. Cook at 170ºC for 10 minutes
6. At the halfway point, sprinkle the cheese on top
7. Loosen the edges with a spatula before serving

Easy Cheese & Bacon Toasties

Servings: 2

Ingredients:

- 4 slices of sandwich bread
- 2 slices of cheddar cheese
- 5 slices of pre-cooked bacon
- 1 tbsp melted butter
- 2 slices of mozzarella cheese

Directions:

1. Take the bread and spread the butter onto one side of each slice
2. Place one slice of bread into the fryer basket, buttered side facing downwards
3. Place the cheddar on top, followed by the bacon, mozzarella and the other slice of bread on top, buttered side upwards
4. Set your fryer to 170ºC
5. Cook for 4 minutes and then turn over and cook for another 3 minutes
6. Serve whilst still hot

French Toast Slices

Servings: 1

Ingredients:

- 2 eggs
- 5 slices sandwich bread
- 100ml milk
- 2 tbsp flour
- 3 tbsp sugar
- 1 tsp ground cinnamon
- 1/2 tsp vanilla extract
- Pinch of salt

Directions:

1. Preheat your air fryer to 220ºC
2. Take your bread and cut it into three pieces of the same size
3. Take a mixing bowl and combine the other ingredients until smooth
4. Dip the bread into the mixture, coating evenly
5. Take a piece of parchment paper and lay it inside the air fryer
6. Arrange the bread on the parchment paper in one layer
7. Cook for 5 minutes
8. Turn and cook for another 5 minutes

European Pancakes

Servings: 5

Ingredients:

- 3 large eggs
- 130g flour
- 140ml whole milk
- 2 tbsp unsweetened apple sauce
- A pinch of salt

Directions:

1. Set your fryer to 200°C and add five ramekins inside to heat up
2. Place all your ingredients inside a blender to combine
3. Spray the ramekins with a little cooking spray
4. Pour the batter into the ramekins carefully
5. Fry for between 6-8 minutes, depending on your preference
6. Serve with your favourite toppings

Breakfast Sausage Burgers

Servings: 2

Ingredients:

- 8 links of your favourite sausage
- Salt and pepper to taste

Directions:

1. Remove the sausage from the skins and use a fork to create a smooth mixture
2. Season to your liking
3. Shape the sausage mixture into burgers or patties
4. Preheat your air fryer to 260°C
5. Arrange the burgers in the fryer, so they are not touching each other
6. Cook for 8 minutes
7. Serve still warm

Poultry Recipes

Poultry Recipes

Hawaiian Chicken

Servings: 2

Ingredients:

- 2 chicken breasts
- 1 tbsp butter
- A pinch of salt and pepper
- 160ml pineapple juice
- 25g brown sugar
- 3 tbsp soy sauce
- 2 tsp water
- 1 clove of garlic, minced
- 1 tsp grated ginger
- 2 tsp cornstarch

Directions:

1. Preheat the air fryer to 260°C
2. Take a bowl and combine the butter and salt and pepper
3. Cover the chicken with the butter and cook in the fryer for 15 minutes, turning halfway
4. Remove and allow to rest for 5 minutes
5. Take another bowl and mix together the pineapple juice, soy sauce, garlic, ginger, and brown sugar
6. Transfer to a saucepan and simmer for 5 minutes
7. Combine the water and cornstarch and add to the sauce, stirring continually for another minute
8. Slice the chicken into strips and pour the sauce over the top

Orange Chicken

Servings: 2

Ingredients:

- 600g chicken thighs, boneless and skinless
- 2 tbsp cornstarch
- 60ml orange juice
- 1 tbsp soy sauce
- 2 tbsp brown sugar
- 1 tbsp rice wine vinegar
- 1/4 teaspoon ground ginger
- Pinch of red pepper flakes
- Zest of one orange
- 2 tsp water and 2 tsp cornstarch mixed together

Directions:

1. Preheat your air fryer to 250°C
2. Take a bowl and combine the chicken with the cornstarch
3. Place in the air fryer and cook for 9 minutes
4. Take a bowl and combine the rest of the ingredients, except for the water and cornstarch mixture
5. Place in a saucepan and bring to the boil and then turn down to a simmer for 5 minutes
6. Add the water and cornstarch mixture to the pan and combine well
7. Remove the chicken from the fryer and pour the sauce over the top

Chicken & Potatoes

Servings: 4

Ingredients:

- 2 tbsp olive oil
- 2 potatoes, cut into 2" pieces
- 2 chicken breasts, cut into pieces of around 1" size
- 4 crushed garlic cloves
- 2 tsp smoked paprika
- 1 tsp thyme
- 1/2 tsp red chilli flakes
- Salt and pepper to taste

Directions:

1. Preheat your air fryer to 260°C
2. Take a large bowl and combine the potatoes with half of the garlic, half the paprika, half the chilli flakes, salt, pepper and half the oil
3. Place into the air fryer and cook for 5 minutes, before turning over and cooking for another 5 minutes
4. Take a bowl and add the chicken with the rest of the seasonings and oil, until totally coated
5. Add the chicken to the potatoes mixture, moving the potatoes to the side
6. Cook for 10 minutes, turning the chicken halfway through

Charred Chicken Breasts

Servings: 2

Ingredients:

- 2 tsp paprika
- 1 tsp ground thyme
- 1 tsp cumin
- ½ tsp cayenne pepper
- ½ tsp onion powder
- ½ tsp black pepper
- ¼ tsp salt
- 2 tsp vegetable oil
- 2 skinless boneless chicken breasts, cut into halves

Directions:

1. Take a bowl and add the paprika, thyme, cumin, cayenne pepper, onion powder, black pepper and salt
2. Coat each chicken breast with oil and dredge chicken in the spice mixture
3. Preheat air fryer to 175C
4. Cook for 10 minutes and flip
5. Cook for 10 more minutes

Whole Chicken

Servings: 4

Ingredients:

- 1.5-kg/3¼-lb. chicken
- 2 tablespoons butter or coconut oil
- salt and freshly ground black pepper

Directions:

1. Place the chicken breast-side up and carefully insert the butter or oil between the skin and the flesh of each breast. Season.
2. Preheat the air-fryer to 180°C/350°F. If the chicken hits the heating element, remove the drawer to lower the chicken a level.
3. Add the chicken to the preheated air-fryer breast-side up. Air-fry for 30 minutes, then turn over and cook for a further 10 minutes. Check the internal temperature with a meat thermometer. If it is 75°C/167°F at the thickest part, remove the chicken from the air-fryer and leave to rest for 10 minutes before carving. If less than 75°C/167°F, continue to cook until this internal temperature is reached and then allow to rest.

Turkey And Mushroom Burgers

Servings: 2

Ingredients:

- 180g mushrooms
- 500g minced turkey
- 1 tbsp of your favourite chicken seasoning, e.g. Maggi
- 1 tsp onion powder
- 1 tsp garlic powder
- Salt and pepper to taste

Directions:

1. Place the mushrooms in a food processor and puree
2. Add all the seasonings and mix well
3. Remove from the food processor and transfer to a mixing bowl
4. Add the minced turkey and combine again
5. Shape the mix into 5 burger patties
6. Spray with cooking spray and place in the air fryer
7. Cook at 160°C for 10 minutes, until cooked.

Chicken Tikka

Servings: 2

Ingredients:

- 2 chicken breasts, diced
- FIRST MARINADE
- freshly squeezed juice of ½ a lemon
- 1 tablespoon freshly grated ginger
- 1 tablespoon freshly grated garlic
- a good pinch of salt
- SECOND MARINADE
- 100 g/½ cup Greek yogurt
- ½ teaspoon chilli powder
- ½ teaspoon chilli paste
- ½ teaspoon turmeric
- ½ teaspoon garam masala
- 1 tablespoon olive oil

Directions:

1. Mix the ingredients for the first marinade together in a bowl, add in the chicken and stir to coat all the chicken pieces. Leave in the fridge to marinate for 20 minutes.
2. Combine the second marinade ingredients. Once the first marinade has had 20 minutes, add the second marinade to the chicken and stir well. Leave in the fridge for at least 4 hours.
3. Preheat the air-fryer to 180°C/350°F.
4. Thread the chicken pieces onto metal skewers that fit in your air-fryer. Add the skewers to the preheated air-fryer and air-fry for 10 minutes. Check the internal temperature of the chicken has reached at least 74°C/165°F using a meat thermometer – if not, cook for another few minutes and then serve.

Healthy Bang Bang Chicken

Servings: 4

Ingredients:

- 500g chicken breasts, cut into pieces of around 1" in size
- 1 beaten egg
- 50ml milk
- 1 tbsp hot pepper sauce
- 80g flour
- 70g tapioca starch
- 1 ½ tsp seasoned starch
- 1 tsp garlic granules
- ½ tsp cumin
- 6 tbsp plain Greek yogurt
- 3 tbsp sweet chilli sauce
- 1 tsp hot sauce

Directions:

1. Preheat the air fryer to 190°C
2. Take a mixing bowl and combine the egg, milk and hot sauce
3. Take another bowl and combine the flour, tapioca starch, salt, garlic and cumin
4. Dip the chicken pieces into the sauce bowl and then into the flour bowl
5. Place the chicken into the air fryer
6. Whilst cooking, mix together the Greek yogurt, sweet chilli sauce and hot sauce and serve with the chicken

Air Fryer Sesame Chicken Thighs

Servings: 4

Ingredients:

- 2 tbsp sesame oil
- 2 tbsp soy sauce
- 1 tbsp honey
- 1 tbsp sriracha sauce
- 1 tsp rice vinegar
- 400g chicken thighs
- 1 green onion, chopped
- 2 tbsp toasted sesame seeds

Directions:

1. Take a large bowl and combine the sesame oil, soy sauce, honey, sriracha and vinegar
2. Add the chicken and refrigerate for 30 minutes
3. Preheat the air fryer to 200°C
4. Cook for 5 minutes
5. Flip and then cook for another 10 minutes
6. Serve with green onion and sesame seeds

Chicken Parmesan With Marinara Sauce

Servings: 4

Ingredients:

- 400g chicken breasts, sliced in half
- 250g panko breadcrumbs
- 140g grated parmesan cheese
- 140g grated mozzarella cheese
- 3 egg whites
- 200g marinara sauce
- 2 tsp Italian seasoning
- Salt and pepper to taste
- Cooking spray

Directions:

1. Preheat the air fryer to 200°C
2. Lay the chicken slices on the work surface and pound with a mallet or a rolling pin to flatten
3. Take a mixing bowl and add the panko breadcrumbs, cheese and the seasoning, combining well
4. Add the egg whites into a separate bowl
5. Dip the chicken into the egg whites and then the breadcrumbs
6. Cook for 7 minutes in the air fryer

Buffalo Wings

Servings: 4

Ingredients:
- 500g chicken wings
- 1 tbsp olive oil
- 5 tbsp cayenne pepper sauce
- 75g butter
- 2 tbsp vinegar
- 1 tsp garlic powder
- ¼ tsp cayenne pepper

Directions:
1. Preheat the air fryer to 182C
2. Take a large mixing bowl and add the chicken wings
3. Drizzle oil over the wings, coating evenly
4. Cook for 25 minutes and then flip the wings and cook for 5 more minutes
5. In a saucepan over a medium heat, mix the hot pepper sauce, butter, vinegar, garlic powder and cayenne pepper, combining well
6. Pour the sauce over the wings and flip to coat, before serving

Chicken Kiev

Servings: 4

Ingredients:
- 4 boneless chicken breasts
- 4 tablespoons plain/all-purpose flour (gluten-free if you wish)
- 1 egg, beaten
- 130 g/2 cups dried breadcrumbs (gluten-free if you wish, see page 9)
- GARLIC BUTTER
- 60 g/4 tablespoons salted butter, softened
- 1 large garlic clove, finely chopped

Directions:

1. Mash together the butter and garlic. Form into a sausage shape, then slice into 4 equal discs. Place in the freezer until frozen.

2. Make a deep horizontal slit across each chicken breast, taking care not to cut through to the other side. Stuff the cavity with a disc of frozen garlic butter. Place the flour in a shallow bowl, the egg in another and the breadcrumbs in a third. Coat each chicken breast first in flour, then egg, then breadcrumbs.

3. Preheat the air-fryer to 180ºC/350ºF.

4. Add the chicken Kievs to the preheated air-fryer and air-fry for 12 minutes until cooked through. This is hard to gauge as the butter inside the breast is not an indicator of doneness, so test the meat in the centre with a meat thermometer – it should be at least 75ºC/167ºF; if not, cook for another few minutes.

Servings: 4

Ingredients:

- 100g tikka masala curry pasta
- 200g low fat yogurt
- 600g skinless chicken breasts
- 1 tbsp vegetable oil
- 1 onion, chopped
- 400g can of the whole, peeled tomatoes
- 20ml water
- 1 tbsp sugar
- 2 tbsp lemon juice
- 1 small bunch of chopped coriander leaves

Directions:

1. Take a bowl and combine the tikka masala curry paste with half the yogurt
2. Cut the chicken into strips
3. Preheat the air fryer to 200ºC
4. Add the yogurt mixture and coat the chicken until fully covered
5. Place into the refrigerator for 2 hours
6. Place the oil and onion in the air fryer and cook for 10 minutes
7. Add the marinated chicken, tomatoes, water and the rest of the yogurt and combine
8. Add the sugar and lemon juice and combine again
9. Cook for 15 minutes

Satay Chicken Skewers

Servings: 4

Ingredients:

- 3 chicken breasts, chopped into 3 x 3-cm/1¼ x 1¼-in. cubes
- MARINADE
- 200 ml/¾ cup canned coconut milk (including the thick part from the can)
- 1 plump garlic clove, finely chopped
- 2 teaspoons freshly grated ginger
- 2 tablespoons soy sauce
- 1 heaped tablespoon peanut butter
- 1 tablespoon maple syrup
- 1 tablespoon mild curry powder
- 1 tablespoon fish sauce

Directions:

1. Mix the marinade ingredients thoroughly in a bowl, then toss in the chopped chicken and stir to coat thoroughly. Leave in the fridge to marinate for at least 4 hours.

2. Preheat the air-fryer to 190ºC/375ºF.

3. Thread the chicken onto 8 metal skewers. Add to the preheated air-fryer (you may need to cook these in two batches, depending on the size of your air-fryer). Air-fry for 10 minutes. Check the internal temperature of the chicken has reached at least 74ºC/165ºF using a meat thermometer – if not, cook for another few minutes and then serve.

Air Fried Maple Chicken Thighs

Servings: 4

Ingredients:

- 200ml buttermilk
- ½ tbsp maple syrup
- 1 egg
- 1 tsp granulated garlic salt
- 4 chicken thighs with the bone in
- 140g all purpose flour
- 65g tapioca flour

- 1 tsp sweet paprika
- 1 tsp onion powder
- ¼ tsp ground black pepper
- ¼ tsp cayenne pepper
- ½ tsp granulated garlic
- ½ tsp honey powder

Directions:

1. Take a bowl and combine the buttermilk, maple syrup, egg and garlic powder
2. Transfer to a bag and add chicken thighs, shaking to combine well
3. Set aside for 1 hour
4. Take a shallow bowl and add the flour, tapioca flour, salt, sweet paprika, smoked paprika, pepper, cayenne pepper and honey powder, combining well
5. Preheat the air fryer to 190°C
6. Drag the chicken through flour mixture and place the chicken skin side down in the air fryer Cook for 12 minutes, until white in the middle

Quick Chicken Nuggets

Servings: 4

Ingredients:

- 500g chicken tenders
- 25g ranch salad dressing mixture
- 2 tbsp plain flour
- 100g breadcrumbs
- 1 egg, beaten
- Olive oil spray

Directions:

1. Take a large mixing bowl and arrange the chicken inside
2. Sprinkle the seasoning over the top and ensure the chicken is evenly coated
3. Place the chicken to one side for around 10 minutes
4. Add the flour into a resealable bag
5. Crack the egg into a small mixing bowl and whisk
6. Pour the breadcrumbs onto a medium sized plate
7. Transfer the chicken into the resealable bag and coat with the flour, giving it a good shake
8. Remove the chicken and dip into the egg, and then rolling it into the breadcrumbs, coating evenly
9. Repeat with all pieces of the chicken
10. Heat your air fryer to 200°C
11. Arrange the chicken inside the fryer and add a little olive oil spray to avoid sticking
12. Cook for 4 minutes, before turning over and cooking for another 4 minutes
13. Remove and serve whilst hot

Chicken And Cheese Chimichangas

Servings: 6

Ingredients:

- 100g shredded chicken (cooked)
- 150g nacho cheese
- 1 chopped jalapeño pepper
- 6 flour tortillas
- 5 tbsp salsa
- 60g refried beans
- 1 tsp cumin
- 0.5 tsp chill powder
- Salt and pepper to taste

Directions:

1. Take a large mixing bowl and add all of the ingredients, combining well
2. Add ⅓ of the filling to each tortilla and roll into a burrito shape
3. Spray the air fryer with cooking spray and heat to 200°C
4. Place the chimichangas in the air fryer and cook for 7 minutes

Buffalo Chicken Wontons

Servings: 6

Ingredients:

- 200g shredded chicken
- 1 tbsp buffalo sauce
- 4 tbsp softened cream cheese
- 1 sliced spring onion
- 2 tbsp blue cheese crumbles
- 12 wonton wrappers

Directions:

1. Preheat the air fryer to 200°C
2. Take a bowl and combine the chicken and buffalo sauce
3. In another bowl mix the cream cheese until a smooth consistency has formed and then combine the scallion blue cheese and seasoned chicken
4. Take the wonton wrappers and run wet fingers along each edge
5. Place 1 tbsp of the filling into the centre of the wonton and fold the corners together
6. Cook at 200°C for 3 to 5 minutes, until golden brown

Chicken Milanese

Servings: 4

Ingredients:
- 130 g/1¾ cups dried breadcrumbs (gluten-free if you wish, see page 9)
- 50 g/⅔ cup grated Parmesan
- 1 teaspoon dried basil
- ½ teaspoon dried thyme
- ¼ teaspoon freshly ground black pepper
- 1 egg, beaten
- 4 tablespoons plain/all-purpose flour (gluten-free if you wish)
- 4 boneless chicken breasts

Directions:

1. Combine the breadcrumbs, cheese, herbs and pepper in a bowl. In a second bowl beat the egg, and in the third bowl have the plain/all-purpose flour. Dip each chicken breast first into the flour, then the egg, then the seasoned breadcrumbs.
2. Preheat the air-fryer to 180°C/350°F.
3. Add the breaded chicken breasts to the preheated air-fryer and air-fry for 12 minutes. Check the internal temperature of the chicken has reached at least 74°C/165°F using a meat thermometer – if not, cook for another few minutes.

Honey Cajun Chicken Thighs

Servings: 6

Ingredients:
- 100ml buttermilk
- 1 tsp hot sauce
- 400g skinless, boneless chicken thighs
- 150g all purpose flour
- 60g tapioca flour
- 2.5 tsp cajun seasoning
- ½ tsp garlic salt
- ½ tsp honey powder
- ¼ tsp ground paprika
- ⅛ tsp cayenne pepper
- 4 tsp honey

Directions:

1. Take a large bowl and combine the buttermilk and hot sauce
2. Transfer to a plastic bag and add the chicken thighs
3. Allow to marinate for 30 minutes
4. Take another bowl and add the flour, tapioca flour, cajun seasoning, garlic, salt, honey powder, paprika, and cayenne pepper, combining well
5. Dredge the chicken through the mixture
6. Preheat the air fryer to 175C
7. Cook for 15 minutes before flipping the thighs over and cooking for another 10 minutes
8. Drizzle 1 tsp of honey over each thigh

Keto Tandoori Chicken

Servings: 2

Ingredients:
- 500g chicken tenders, halved
- 1 tbsp minced ginger
- 1 tbsp minced garlic
- 1 tsp cayenne pepper
- 1 tsp turmeric
- 1 tsp garam masala
- 60ml yogurt
- 25g coriander leaves
- Salt and pepper to taste

Directions:
1. Take a large mixing bowl and combine all the ingredients, except the chicken
2. Once combined, add the chicken to the bowl and make sure it is fully coated
3. Preheat the air fryer to 160°C
4. Place the chicken in the air fryer and baste with oil
5. Cook for 10 minutes, turning over and then cooking for another 5 minutes
6. Serve whilst still warm

Spicy Chicken Wing Drummettes

Servings: 4

Ingredients:
- 10 large chicken drumettes
- Cooking spray
- 100ml rice vinegar
- 3 tbsp honey
- 2 tbsp unsalted chicken stock
- 1 tbsp lower sodium soy sauce
- 1 tbsp toasted sesame oil
- ⅜ tsp crushed red pepper
- 1 garlic clove, finely chopped
- 2 tbsp chopped, unsalted, roasted peanuts
- 1 tbsp chopped fresh chives

Directions:
1. Coat the chicken in cooking spray and place inside the air fryer
2. Cook at 200°C for 30 minutes
3. Take a mixing bowl and combine the vinegar, honey, stock, soy sauce, oil, crushed red pepper and garlic
4. Cook to a simmer, until a syrup consistency is achieved
5. Coat the chicken in this mixture and sprinkle with peanuts and chives

Beef & Lamb And Pork Recipes

Beef & Lamb And Pork Recipes

Sausage Gnocchi One Pot

Servings: 2

Ingredients:

- 4 links of sausage
- 250g green beans, washed and cut into halves
- 1 tsp Italian seasoning
- 1 tbsp olive oil
- 300g gnocchi
- Salt and pepper for seasoning

Directions:

1. Preheat the air fryer to 220°C
2. Cut the sausage up into pieces
3. Take a bowl and add the gnocchi and green beans, along with the oil and season
4. Place the sausage into the fryer first and then the rest of the ingredients
5. Cook for 12 minutes, giving everything a stir halfway through

Lamb Burgers

Servings: 4

Ingredients:

- 600g minced lamb
- 2 tsp garlic puree
- 1 tsp harissa paste
- 2 tbsp Moroccan spice
- Salt and pepper

Directions:

1. Place all the ingredients in a bowl and mix well
2. Form into patties
3. Place in the air fryer and cook at 180°C for 18 minutes

Pork Chops With Sprouts

Servings: 2

Ingredients:

- 300g pork chops
- ⅛ tsp salt
- ½ tsp pepper
- 250g Brussels sprouts quartered
- 1 tsp olive oil
- 1 tsp maple syrup
- 1 tsp dijon mustard

Directions:

1. Season the pork chops with salt and pepper
2. Mix together oil, maple syrup and mustard. Add Brussels sprouts
3. Add pork chops and Brussels sprouts to the air fryer and cook at 200ºC for about 10 minutes

Kheema Meatloaf

Servings: 4

Ingredients:

- 500g minced beef
- 2 eggs
- 1 diced onion
- 200g sliced coriander
- 1 tbsp minced ginger
- ⅛ cardamom pod
- 1 tbsp minced garlic
- 2 tsp garam masala
- 1 tsp salt
- 1 tsp cayenne
- 1 tsp turmeric
- ½ tsp cinnamon

Directions:

1. Place all the ingredients in a large bowl and mix well
2. Place meat in an 8 inch pan and set air fryer to 180ºC
3. Place in the air fryer and cook for 15 minutes
4. Slice and serve

Lamb Calzone

Servings: 2

Ingredients:

- 1 tsp olive oil
- 1 chopped onion
- 100g baby spinach leaves
- 400g minced pork
- 250g whole wheat pizza dough
- 300g grated cheese

Directions:

1. Heat the olive oil in a pan, add the onion and cook for about 2 minutes
2. Add the spinach and cook for a further 1 ½ minutes
3. Stir in marinara sauce and the minced pork
4. Divide the dough into four and roll out into circles
5. Add ¼ of filling to each piece of dough
6. Sprinkle with cheese and fold the dough over to create half moons, crimp edges to seal
7. Spray with cooking spray, place in the air fryer and cook at 160ºC for 12 minutes turning after 8 minutes

Italian Meatballs

Servings: 12

Ingredients:

- 2 tbsp olive oil
- 2 tbsp minced shallot
- 3 cloves garlic minced
- 100g panko crumbs
- 35g chopped parsley
- 1 tbsp chopped rosemary
- 60ml milk
- 400g minced pork
- 250g turkey sausage
- 1 egg beaten
- 1 tbsp dijon mustard
- 1 tbsp finely chopped thyme

Directions:

1. Preheat air fryer to 200°C
2. Heat oil in a pan and cook the garlic and shallot over a medium heat for 1-2 minutes
3. Mix the panko and milk in a bowl and allow to stand for 5 minutes
4. Add all the ingredients to the panko mix and combine well
5. Shape into 1 ½ inch meatballs and cook for 12 minutes

Beef Stroganoff

Servings:4 | Cooking Time:20 Minutes

Ingredients:

- 4 cubes / 800 ml beef stock cubes
- 4 tbsp olive oil
- 1 onion, chopped
- 200 g / 7 oz sour cream
- 200 g / 7 oz mushroom, finely sliced
- 500 g / 17.6 oz steak, chopped
- 4 x 100 g / 3.5 oz egg noodles, cooked

Directions:

1. Preheat the air fryer to 200 °C / 400 °F and line the bottom of the basket with parchment paper.
2. Boil 800 ml of water and use it to dissolve the 4 beef stock cubes.
3. In a heat-proof bowl, mix the olive oil, onion, sour cream, mushrooms, and beef stock until fully combined.
4. Coat all sides of the steak chunks in the mixture and set aside to marinate for 10 minutes.
5. Transfer the steak to the air fryer, close the lid, and cook for 10 minutes. Serve the steak hot with a serving of egg noodles.

Steak Dinner

Servings: 5

Ingredients:

- 400g sirloin steak, cut into cubes
- 300g red potatoes, cubed
- 1 pepper
- 1 tsp dried parsley
- ½ tsp pepper
- 2 tsp olive oil
- 1 sliced onion
- 300g chopped mushrooms
- 2 tsp garlic salt
- 2 tsp salt
- 5 tsp butter

Directions:

1. Preheat the air fryer to 200ºC
2. Take 5 pieces of foil, layer meat onion, potatoes, mushrooms and pepper in each one
3. Add 1 tsp of butter to each one
4. Mix seasonings and sprinkle over the top
5. Fold the foil and cook for 25-30 minutes

Meatballs In Tomato Sauce

Servings: 4

Ingredients:

- 1 small onion
- 300g minced pork
- 1 tbsp chopped parsley
- 1 tbsp thyme
- 1 egg
- 3 tbsp bread crumbs
- Salt and pepper to taste

Directions:

1. Place all ingredients into a bowl and mix well
2. Shape mixture into 12 meatballs
3. Heat the air fryer to 200ºC
4. Place the meatballs into the air fryer and cook for about 7 minutes
5. Tip the meatballs into an oven dish add the tomato sauce and cook for about 5 minutes in the air fryer until warmed through

Breaded Bone-in Pork Chops

Servings: 2

Ingredients:

- 2 pork chops with the bone in
- 250g Italian breadcrumbs
- 2 tbsp mayonnaise
- 1/2 tsp garlic powder
- 1/2 tsp onion powder
- 1/2 tsp thyme
- 1/2 tsp paprika
- Salt and pepper to taste

Directions:

1. Preheat the air fryer to 260°C
2. Take a large bowl and add the breadcrumbs, garlic powder, paprika, salt and pepper, and thyme, and onion powder, combining well
3. Cover the pork chops with the mayonnaise making sure to cover both sides
4. Coat the meat with the seasoning mixture, making sure it is fully covered
5. Cook the pork chops in the fryer for 10 minutes, turning over halfway

Buttermilk Pork Chops

Servings: 4

Ingredients:

- 4 pork chops
- 3 tbsp buttermilk
- 75g flour
- Cooking oil spray
- 1 packet of pork rub
- Salt and pepper to taste

Directions:

1. Rub the chops with the pork rub
2. Place the pork chops in a bowl and drizzle with buttermilk
3. Coat the chops with flour
4. Place in the air fryer and cook at 190°C for 15 minutes turning halfway

Pulled Pork, Bacon, And Cheese Sliders

Servings:2 | Cooking Time:30 Minutes

Ingredients:

- 2 x 50 g / 3.5 oz pork steaks
- 1 tsp salt
- 1 tsp black pepper
- 4 slices bacon strips, chopped into small pieces
- 1 tbsp soy sauce
- 1 tbsp BBQ sauce
- 100 g / 7 oz cheddar cheese, grated
- 2 bread buns

Directions:

1. Preheat the air fryer to 200 °C / 400 °F and line the bottom of the basket with parchment paper.
2. Place the pork steaks on a clean surface and season with salt and black pepper. Move the pork steak in the prepared air fryer basket and cook for 15 minutes.
3. Remove the steak from the air fryer and shred using two forks. Mix with the chopped bacon in a heatproof bowl and place the bowl in the air fryer. Cook for 10 minutes.
4. Remove the bowl from the air fryer and stir in the soy sauce and BBQ sauce. Return the bowl to the air fryer basket and continue cooking for a further 5 minutes.
5. Meanwhile, spread the cheese across one half of the bread buns. Top with the cooked pulled pork and an extra squirt of BBQ sauce.

Pork Taquitos

Servings: 5

Ingredients:

- 400g shredded pork
- 500g grated mozzarella
- 10 flour tortillas
- The juice of 1 lime
- Cooking spray

Directions:

1. Preheat air fryer to 190ºC
2. Sprinkle lime juice on the pork and mix
3. Microwave tortilla for about 10 seconds to soften
4. Add a little pork and cheese to a tortilla
5. Roll then tortilla up, and place in the air fryer
6. Cook for about 7 minutes until golden, turn halfway through cooking

Parmesan Crusted Pork Chops

Servings: 6

Ingredients:
- 6 pork chops
- ½ tsp salt
- ¼ tsp pepper
- 1 tsp paprika
- 3 tbsp parmesan
- ½ tsp onion powder
- ¼ tsp chilli powder
- 2 eggs beaten
- 250g pork rind crumbs

Directions:
1. Preheat the air fryer to 200ºC
2. Season the pork with the seasonings
3. Place the pork rind into a food processor and blend into crumbs
4. Mix the pork rind and seasonings in a bowl
5. Beat the eggs in a separate bowl
6. Dip the pork into the egg then into the crumb mix
7. Place pork in the air fryer and cook for about 15 minutes until crispy

Pork Belly With Crackling

Servings: 4

Ingredients:
- 800g belly pork
- 1 tsp sea salt
- 1 tsp garlic salt
- 2 tsp five spice
- 1 tsp rosemary
- 1 tsp white pepper
- 1 tsp sugar
- Half a lemon

Directions:
1. Cut lines into the meat portion of the belly pork
2. Cook thoroughly in water
3. Allow to air dry for 3 hours
4. Score the skin and prick holes with a fork
5. Rub with the dry rub mix, rub some lemon juice on the skin
6. Place in the air fryer and cook at 160ºC for 30 minutes then at 180ºC for a further 30 minutes

Beef Stirfry

Servings: 2

Ingredients:

- 500g steak
- 400g broccoli
- 3 peppers, cut into strips
- 1 tbsp ground ginger
- 25ml water
- 1 sliced onion
- 25g hoisin sauce
- 2 tsp minced garlic
- 1 tsp sesame oil
- 1 tbsp soy

Directions:

1. Add sesame oil, hoisin sauce, garlic, soy and water to a bowl and then add the steak, allow to marinate for 20 minutes
2. Mix 1 tbsp of oil with the vegetables and place in the air fryer, cook at 200ºC for about 5 minutes
3. Place the vegetables in a bowl and put aside
4. Add meat to air fryer and cook for 4 minutes, turn and cook for a further 2 minutes
5. Mix the steak with the vegetables and serve with rice

Steak Popcorn Bites

Servings: 4

Ingredients:

- 500g steak, cut into 1" sized cubes
- 500g potato chips, ridged ones work best
- 100g flour
- 2 beaten eggs
- Salt and pepper to taste

Directions:

1. Place the chips into the food processor and pulse unit you get fine chip crumbs
2. Take a bowl and combine the flour with salt and pepper
3. Add the chips to another bowl and the beaten egg to another bowl
4. Take the steak cubes and dip first in the flour, then the egg and then the chip crumbs
5. Preheat your air fryer to 260ºC
6. Place the steak pieces into the fryer and cook for 9 minutes

Mongolian Beef

Servings: 4

Ingredients:

- 500g steak
- 25g cornstarch
- 2 tsp vegetable oil
- ½ tsp ginger
- 1 tbsp garlic minced
- 75g soy sauce
- 75g water
- 100g brown sugar

Directions:

1. Slice the steak and coat in corn starch
2. Place in the air fryer and cook at 200ºC for 10 minutes turning halfway
3. Place remaining ingredients in a sauce pan and gently warm
4. When cooked place the steak in a bowl and pour the sauce over

Sausage Burritos

Servings:4 | Cooking Time:20 Minutes

Ingredients:

- 1 medium sweet potato
- 2 tbsp olive oil
- 1 tsp salt
- 1 tsp black pepper
- 8 sausages, uncooked
- 4 white flour tortillas
- 4 eggs, beaten
- 200 ml milk (any kind)
- 100 g / 3.5 oz cheddar cheese, grated

Directions:

1. Preheat the air fryer to 200 °C / 400 °F and line the air fryer mesh basket with parchment paper.
2. Peel the sweet potato and cut it into small chunks.
3. Place the sweet potato chunks in a bowl and toss in 1 tbsp olive oil. Sprinkle salt and pepper over the top.
4. Transfer the sweet potato chunks into the air fryer and cook for 8-10 minutes until hot. Remove from the air fryer and set aside to drain on paper towels.
5. Heat 1 tbsp olive oil in a medium frying pan and cook the sausages for 5-7 minutes until slightly browned. Remove the sausages and set them aside on paper towels to drain.
6. In a bowl, whisk together the beaten eggs and milk, and pour into the hot frying pan. Cook the eggs and use a fork to scramble them as they cook in the pan.
7. Once the eggs are cooked, mix them with the potatoes, sausages, and cheddar cheese in a bowl.
8. Spread the mixture evenly across the 4 white flour tortillas and roll them each up into tight burritos. Use a toothpick to keep them together if necessary.
9. Place the burritos into the hot air fryer and cook for 6-8 minutes, turning them over halfway through.
10. Enjoy the burritos for breakfast or lunch.

Pork Schnitzel

Servings: 2

Ingredients:

- 3 pork steaks, cut into cubes
- Salt and pepper
- 175g flour
- 2 eggs
- 175g breadcrumbs

Directions:

1. Sprinkle the pork with salt and pepper
2. Coat in the flour then dip in the egg
3. Coat the pork in breadcrumbs
4. Place in the air fryer and cook at 175°C for 20 minutes turning halfway
5. Serve with red cabbage

Sweet And Sticky Ribs

Servings:2 | Cooking Time:1 Hour 15 Minutes

Ingredients:

- 500 g / 17.6 oz pork ribs
- 2 cloves garlic, minced
- 2 tbsp soy sauce
- 2 tsp honey
- 1 tbsp cayenne pepper
- 1 tsp olive oil
- 2 tbsp BBQ sauce
- 1 tsp salt
- 1 tsp black pepper

Directions:

1. Place the pork ribs on a clean surface and cut them into smaller chunks if necessary.
2. In a small mixing bowl, combine the minced garlic, soy sauce, 1 tsp honey, cayenne pepper, olive oil, BBQ sauce, salt, and pepper. Rub the pork ribs into the sauce and spice the mixture until fully coated.
3. Place the coated ribs in the fridge for 1 hour. Meanwhile, preheat the air fryer to 180 °C / 350 °F and line the bottom of the basket with parchment paper.
4. After one hour, transfer the pork ribs into the prepared air fryer basket. Close the lid and cook for 15 minutes, using tongs to turn them halfway through.
5. Once cooked, remove the ribs from the air fryer and use a brush to top each rib with the remaining 1 tsp honey.
6. Return the ribs to the air fryer for a further 2-3 minutes to heat the honey glaze before serving.

Fillet Mignon Wrapped In Bacon

Servings: 2

Ingredients:

- 1 kg filet mignon
- 500g bacon slices
- Olive oil

Directions:

1. Wrap the fillets in bacon
2. Season with salt and pepper and brush with olive oil
3. Place in the air fryer cook at 200°C for 9 minutes turning halfway through

Fish & Seafood Recipes

Shrimp With Yum Yum Sauce

Servings: 4

Ingredients:

- 400g peeled jumbo shrimp
- 1 tbsp soy sauce
- 1 tbsp garlic paste
- 1 tbsp ginger paste
- 4 tbsp mayo
- 2 tbsp ketchup
- 1 tbsp sugar
- 1 tsp paprika
- 1 tsp garlic powder

Directions:

1. Mix soy sauce, garlic paste and ginger paste in a bowl. Add the shrimp, allow to marinate for 15 minutes
2. In another bowl mix ketchup, mayo, sugar, paprika and the garlic powder to make the yum yum sauce.
3. Set the air fryer to 200ºC, place shrimp in the basket and cook for 8-10 minutes

Cajun Shrimp Boil

Servings: 6

Ingredients:

- 300g cooked shrimp
- 14 slices of smoked sausage
- 5 par boiled potatoes, cut into halves
- 4 mini corn on the cobs, quartered
- 1 diced onion
- 3 tbsp old bay seasoning
- Olive oil spray

Directions:

1. Combine all the ingredients in a bowl and mix well
2. Line the air fryer with foil
3. Place half the mix into the air fryer and cook at 200ºC for about 6 minutes, mix the ingredients and cook for a further 6 minutes.
4. Repeat for the second batch

Crispy Cajun Fish Fingers

Servings: 2

Ingredients:

- 350 g/12 oz. cod loins
- 1 teaspoon smoked paprika
- ½ teaspoon cayenne pepper
- ½ teaspoon onion granules
- ¾ teaspoon dried oregano
- ¼ teaspoon dried thyme
- ½ teaspoon salt
- ½ teaspoon unrefined sugar
- 40 g/½ cup dried breadcrumbs (gluten-free if you wish, see page 9)
- 2 tablespoons plain/all-purpose flour (gluten-free if you wish)
- 1 egg, beaten

Directions:

1. Slice the cod into 6 equal fish 'fingers'. Mix the spices, herbs, salt and sugar together, then combine with the breadcrumbs. Lay out three bowls: one with flour, one with beaten egg and one with the Cajun-spiced breadcrumbs. Dip each fish finger into the flour, then the egg, then the breadcrumbs until fully coated.
2. Preheat the air-fryer to 180°C/350°F.
3. Add the fish to the preheated air-fryer and air-fry for 6 minutes, until cooked inside. Check the internal temperature of the fish has reached at least 75°C/167°F using a meat thermometer – if not, cook for another few minutes.

Shrimp Wrapped With Bacon

Servings: 2

Ingredients:

- 16 shrimp
- 16 slices of bacon
- 2 tbsp ranch dressing to serve

Directions:

1. Preheat the air fryer to 200°C
2. Wrap the shrimps in the bacon
3. Refrigerate for 30 minutes
4. Cook the shrimp for about 5 minutes turn them over and cook for a further 2 minutes
5. Serve with the ranch dressing on the side

Cod In Parma Ham

Servings: 2

Ingredients:

- 2 x 175–190-g/6–7-oz. cod fillets, skin removed
- 6 slices Parma ham or prosciutto
- 16 cherry tomatoes
- 60 g/2 oz. rocket/arugula
- DRESSING

- 1 tablespoon olive oil
- 1½ teaspoons balsamic vinegar
- garlic salt, to taste
- freshly ground black pepper, to taste

Directions:

1. Preheat the air-fryer to 180ºC/350ºF.
2. Wrap each piece of cod snugly in 3 ham slices. Add the ham-wrapped cod fillets and the tomatoes to the pre-heated air-fryer and air-fry for 6 minutes, turning the cod halfway through cooking. Check the internal temperature of the fish has reached at least 60ºC/140ºF using a meat thermometer – if not, cook for another minute.
3. Meanwhile, make the dressing by combining all the ingredients in a jar and shaking well.
4. Serve the cod and tomatoes on a bed of rocket/arugula with the dressing poured over.

Fish Sticks With Tartar Sauce Batter

Servings: 4

Ingredients:

- 6 tbsp mayonnaise
- 2 tbsp dill pickle
- 1 tsp seafood seasoning

- 400g cod fillets, cut into sticks
- 300g panko breadcrumbs

Directions:

1. Combine the mayonnaise, seafood seasoning and dill pickle in a large bowl.
2. Add the cod sticks and coat well
3. Preheat air fryer to 200ºC
4. Coat the fish sticks in the breadcrumbs
5. Place in the air fryer and cook for 12 minutes

Crispy Nacho Prawns

Servings: 6

Ingredients:

- 1 egg
- 18 large prawns
- 1 bag of nacho cheese flavoured corn chips, crushed

Directions:

1. Wash the prawns and pat dry
2. Place the chips into a bowl
3. In another bowl, whisk the egg
4. Dip the prawns into the egg and then the nachos
5. Preheat the air fryer to 180ºC
6. Cook for 8 minutes

Tandoori Salmon

Servings: 4

Ingredients:
- 300g salmon
- 1 tbsp butter
- 1 tbsp tandoori spice
- Salt and pepper to taste
- 1 small tomato
- Half a red onion
- 600g plain yogurt
- 30 fresh mint leaves, chopped
- 1 tsp minced green chilli
- 1 tbsp ground cumin
- Half a cucumber, chopped

Directions:
1. Cut the salmon into cubes and coat in the tandoori spice mix. Chill for 30 minutes to marinate
2. Blend mint, cumin and chilli with ¼ of the yogurt refrigerate and leave to steep
3. Peel the tomato and cut into cubes. Peel the cucumber and chop into cubes, finely dice the onion
4. Cook the salmon in the air fryer for 5-6 minutes at 200°C
5. Mix the flavoured yogurt with the remaining yogurt, tomato, cucumber and onion
6. Place the sauce in serving bowls and place the salmon on top

Sea Bass With Asparagus Spears

Servings: 2

Ingredients:
- 2 x 100-g/3½-oz. sea bass fillets
- 8 asparagus spears
- 2 teaspoons olive oil
- salt and freshly ground black pepper
- boiled new potatoes, to serve
- CAPER DRESSING
- 1½ tablespoons olive oil
- grated zest and freshly squeezed juice of ½ lemon
- 1 tablespoon small, jarred capers
- 1 teaspoon Dijon mustard
- 1 tablespoon freshly chopped flat-leaf parsley

Directions:
1. Preheat the air-fryer to 180°C/350°F.
2. Prepare the fish and asparagus by brushing both with the olive oil and sprinkling over salt and pepper.
3. Add the asparagus to the preheated air-fryer and air-fry for 4 minutes, then turn the asparagus and add the fish to the air-fryer drawer. Cook for a further 4 minutes. Check the internal temperature of the fish has reached at least 60°C/140°F using a meat thermometer – if not, cook for another minute.
4. Meanwhile, make the dressing by combining all the ingredients in a jar and shaking well. Pour the dressing over the cooked fish and asparagus spears and serve with new potatoes.

Furikake Salmon

Servings: 2

Ingredients:

- 1 salmon fillet
- 2 tbsp furikake
- 150ml mayonnaise
- 1 tbsp shoe
- Salt and pepper for seasoning

Directions:

1. Preheat the air fryer to 230ºC
2. Take a small bowl and combine the mayonnaise and shoyu
3. Add salt and pepper to the salmon on both sides
4. Place in the air fryer with the skin facing downwards
5. Brush a layer of the mayonnaise mixture on top of the salmon
6. Sprinkle the furikake on top
7. Cook for 10 minutes

Fish In Foil

Servings: 2

Ingredients:

- 1 tablespoon avocado oil or olive oil, plus extra for greasing
- 1 tablespoon soy sauce (or tamari)
- 1½ teaspoons freshly grated garlic
- 1½ teaspoons freshly grated ginger
- 1 small red chilli/chile, finely chopped
- 2 skinless, boneless white fish fillets (about 350 g/12 oz. total weight)

Directions:

1. Mix the oil, soy sauce, garlic, ginger and chilli/chile together. Brush a little oil onto two pieces of foil, then lay the fish in the centre of the foil. Spoon the topping mixture over the fish. Wrap the foil around the fish to make a parcel, with a gap above the fish but shallow enough to fit in your air-fryer basket.
2. Preheat the air-fryer to 180ºC/350ºF.
3. Add the foil parcels to the preheated air-fryer and air-fry for 7–10 minutes, depending on the thickness of your fillets. The fish should just flake when a fork is inserted. Serve immediately.

Thai Salmon Patties

Servings: 7

Ingredients:

- 1 large can of salmon, drained and bones removed
- 30g panko breadcrumbs
- ¼ tsp salt
- 1 ½ tbsp Thai red curry paste
- 1 ½ tbsp brown sugar
- Zest of 1 lime
- 2 eggs
- Cooking spray

Directions:

1. Take a large bowl and combine all ingredients together until smooth
2. Use your hands to create patties that are around 1 inch in thickness
3. Preheat your air fryer to 180ºC
4. Coat the patties with cooking spray
5. Cook for 4 minutes each side

Copycat Fish Fingers

Servings: 2

Ingredients:

- 2 slices wholemeal bread, grated into breadcrumbs
- 50g plain flour
- 1 beaten egg
- 1 white fish fillet
- The juice of 1 small lemon
- 1 tsp parsley
- 1 tsp thyme
- 1 tsp mixed herbs
- Salt and pepper to taste

Directions:

1. Preheat the air fryer to 180ºC
2. Add salt pepper and parsley to the breadcrumbs and combine well
3. Place the egg in another bowl
4. Place the flour in a separate bowl
5. Place the fish into a food processor and add the lemon juice, salt, pepper thyme and mixed herbs
6. Blitz to create a crumb-like consistency
7. Roll your fish in the flour, then the egg and then the breadcrumbs
8. Cook at 180ºC for 8 minutes

Honey Sriracha Salmon

Servings: 2

Ingredients:

- 25g sriracha
- 25g honey
- 500g salmon fillets
- 1 tbsp soy sauce

Directions:

1. Mix the honey, soy sauce and sriracha, keep half the mix to one side for dipping
2. Place the salmon in the sauce skin side up and marinade for 30 minutes
3. Spray air fryer basket with cooking spray
4. Heat the air fryer to 200°C
5. Place salmon in the air fryer skin side down and cook for 12 minutes

Garlic Tilapia

Servings: 2

Ingredients:

- 2 tilapia fillets
- 2 tsp chopped fresh chives
- 2 tsp chopped fresh parsley
- 2 tsp olive oil
- 1 tsp minced garlic
- Salt and pepper for seasoning

Directions:

1. Preheat the air fryer to 220°C
2. Take a small bowl and combine the olive oil with the chives, garlic, parsley and a little salt and pepper
3. Brush the mixture over the fish fillets
4. Place the fish into the air fryer and cook for 10 minutes, until flaky

Oat & Parmesan Crusted Fish Fillets

Servings: 2

Ingredients:

- 20 g/⅓ cup fresh breadcrumbs
- 25 g/3 tablespoons oats
- 15 g/¼ cup grated Parmesan
- 1 egg
- 2 x 175-g/6-oz. white fish fillets, skin-on
- salt and freshly ground black pepper

Directions:

1. Preheat the air-fryer to 180°C/350°F.
2. Combine the breadcrumbs, oats and cheese in a bowl and stir in a pinch of salt and pepper. In another bowl beat the egg. Dip the fish fillets in the egg, then top with the oat mixture.
3. Add the fish fillets to the preheated air-fryer on an air-fryer liner or a piece of pierced parchment paper. Air-fry for 10 minutes. Check the fish is just flaking away when a fork is inserted, then serve immediately.

Peppery Lemon Shrimp

Servings: 2

Ingredients:

- 300g uncooked shrimp
- 1 tbsp olive oil
- 1 the juice of 1 lemon
- 0.25 tsp garlic powder
- 1 sliced lemon
- 1 tsp pepper
- 0.25 tsp paprika

Directions:

1. Heat the fryer to 200°C
2. Take a medium sized mixing bowl and combine the lemon juice, pepper, garlic powder, paprika and the olive oil together
3. Add the shrimp to the bowl and make sure they're well coated
4. Arrange the shrimp into the basket of the fryer
5. Cook for between 6-8 minutes, until firm and pink

Garlic Butter Salmon

Servings: 2

Ingredients:

- 2 salmon fillets, boneless with the skin left on
- 1 tsp minced garlic
- 2 tbsp melted butter
- 1 tsp chopped parsley
- Salt and pepper to taste

Directions:

1. Preheat the air fryer to 270 °C
2. Take a bowl and combine the melted butter, parsley and garlic to create a sauce
3. Season the salmon to your liking
4. Brush the salmon with the garlic mixture, on both sides
5. Place the salmon into the fryer, with the skin side facing down
6. Cook for 10 minutes - the salmon is done when it flakes with ease

Crunchy Fish

Servings: 4

Ingredients:

- 200g dry breadcrumbs
- 4 tbsp olive oil
- 4 fillets of white fish
- 1 beaten egg
- 1 sliced lemon

Directions:

1. Heat the fryer to 180ºC
2. In a medium mixing bowl, combine the olive oil and the breadcrumbs
3. Take the fish and first dip it into the egg and then the breadcrumbs, making sure they are evenly coated well
4. Arrange the fish into the basket
5. Cook for 12 minutes
6. Remove and serve with lemon slices

Garlic-parsley Prawns

Servings: 2

Ingredients:

- 300 g/10½ oz. raw king prawns/jumbo shrimp (without shell)
- 40 g/3 tablespoons garlic butter, softened (see page 72)
- 2 tablespoons freshly chopped flat-leaf parsley

Directions:

1. Thread the prawns/shrimp onto 6 metal skewers that will fit your air-fryer. Mix together the softened garlic butter and parsley and brush evenly onto the prawn skewers.

2. Preheat the air-fryer to 180ºC/350ºF.

3. Place the skewers on an air-fryer liner or a piece of pierced parchment paper. Add the skewers to the preheated air-fryer and air-fry for 2 minutes, then turn the skewers over and cook for a further 2 minutes. Check the internal temperature of the prawns has reached at least 50ºC/120ºF using a meat thermometer – if not, cook for another few minutes and serve.

Chilli Lime Tilapia

Servings: 3

Ingredients:
- 500g Tilapia fillets
- 25g panko crumbs
- 200g flour
- Salt and pepper to taste
- 2 eggs
- 1 tbsp chilli powder
- The juice of 1 lime

Directions:
1. Mix panko, salt and pepper and chilli powder together
2. Whisk the egg in a separate bowl
3. Spray the air fryer with cooking spray
4. Dip the tilapia in the flour, then in the egg and cover in the panko mix
5. Place fish in the air fryer, spray with cooking spray and cook for 7-8 minutes at 190°C
6. Turn the fish over and cook for a further 7-8 minutes until golden brown.
7. Squeeze lime juice over the top and serve

Cajun Prawn Skewers

Servings: 2

Ingredients:
- 350 g/12 oz. king prawns/jumbo shrimp
- MARINADE
- 1 teaspoon smoked paprika
- 1 teaspoon unrefined sugar
- 1 teaspoon salt
- ½ teaspoon onion powder
- ½ teaspoon mustard powder
- ¼ teaspoon dried oregano
- ¼ teaspoon dried thyme
- 1 teaspoon white wine vinegar
- 2 teaspoons olive oil

Directions:

1. Mix all the marinade ingredients together in a bowl. Mix the prawns/shrimp into the marinade and cover. Place in the fridge to marinate for at least an hour.

2. Preheat the air-fryer to 180°C/350°F.

3. Thread 4–5 prawns/shrimp on to each skewer (you should have enough for 4–5 skewers). Add the skewers to the preheated air-fryer and air-fry for 2 minutes, then turn the skewers and cook for a further 2 minutes. Check the internal temperature of the prawns/shrimp has reached at least 50°C/125°F using a meat thermometer – if not, cook for another few minutes. Serve immediately.

Vegetarian & Vegan Recipes

Radish Hash Browns

Servings: 4

Ingredients:

- 300g radish
- 1 onion
- 1 tsp onion powder
- ¾ tsp sea salt
- ½ tsp paprika
- ¼ tsp ground black pepper
- 1 tsp coconut oil

Directions:

1. Wash the radish, trim off the roots and slice in a processor along with the onions
2. Add the coconut oil and mix well
3. Put the onions and radish into the air fryer and cook at 180°C for 8 minutes shaking a few times
4. Put the onion and radish in a bowl add seasoning and mix well
5. Put back in the air fryer and cook at 200°C for 5 minutes

Paneer Tikka

Servings: 2

Ingredients:

- 200ml yogurt
- 1 tsp ginger garlic paste
- 1 tsp red chilli powder
- 1 tsp garam masala
- 1 tsp turmeric powder
- 1 tbsp dried fenugreek leaves
- The juice of 1 lemon
- 2 tbsp chopped coriander
- 1 tbsp olive oil
- 250g paneer cheese, cut into cubes
- 1 green pepper, chopped
- 1 red pepper, chopped
- 1 yellow pepper, chopped
- 1 chopped onion

Directions:

1. Take a mixing bowl and add the yogurt, garlic paste, red chilli powder, garam masala, turmeric powder, lemon juice, fenugreek and chopped coriander, combining well
2. Place the marinade to one side
3. Add the cubed cheese to the marinade and toss to coat well
4. Leave to marinade for 2 hours
5. Take 8 skewers and alternate the cheese with the peppers and onions
6. Drizzle a little oil over the top
7. Arrange in the air fryer and cook at 220°C for 3 minutes
8. Turn and cook for another 3 minutes

Spinach And Feta Croissants

Servings:4 | Cooking Time:10 Minutes

Ingredients:

- 4 pre-made croissants
- 100 g / 7 oz feta cheese, crumbled
- 1 tsp dried chives
- 1 tsp garlic powder
- 50 g / 3.5 oz fresh spinach, chopped

Directions:

1. Preheat the air fryer to 180 °C / 350 °F. Remove the mesh basket from the air fryer machine and line with parchment paper.
2. Cut the croissants in half and lay each half out on the lined mesh basket.
3. In a bowl, combine the crumbled feta cheese, dried chives, garlic powder, and chopped spinach until they form a consistent mixture.
4. Spoon some of the mixture one half of the four croissants and cover with the second half of the croissants to seal in the filling.
5. Carefully slide the croissants in the mesh basket into the air fryer machine, close the lid, and cook for 10 minutes until the pastry is crispy and the feta cheese has melted.

Vegan Meatballs

Servings:4 | Cooking Time:15 Minutes

Ingredients:

- 2 tbsp olive oil
- 2 tbsp soy sauce
- 1 onion, finely sliced
- 1 large carrot, peeled and grated
- 1 x 400 g / 14 oz can chickpeas, drained and rinsed
- 50 g / 1.8 oz plain flour
- 50 g / 1.8 oz rolled oats
- 2 tbsp roasted cashews, chopped
- 1 tsp garlic powder
- ½ tsp cumin

Directions:

1. Preheat the air fryer to 175 °C / 350 °F and line the air fryer with parchment paper or grease it with olive oil.
2. In a large mixing bowl, combine the olive oil and soy sauce. Add the onion slices and grated carrot and toss to coat in the sauce.
3. Place the vegetables in the air fryer and cook for 5 minutes until slightly soft.
4. Meanwhile, place the chickpeas, plain flour, rolled oats, and roasted cashews in a blender, and mix until well combined.
5. Remove the mixture from the blender and stir in the garlic powder and cumin. Add the onions and carrots to the bowl and mix well.
6. Scoop the mixture into small meatballs and place them into the air fryer. Increase the temperature on the machine up to 190 °C / 370 °F and cook the meatballs for 10-12 minutes until golden and crispy.

Veggie Bakes

Servings: 2

Ingredients:

- Any type of leftover vegetable bake you have
- 30g flour

Directions:

1. Preheat the air fryer to 180°C
2. Mix the flour with the leftover vegetable bake
3. Shape into balls and place in the air fryer
4. Cook for 10 minutes

Roast Cauliflower & Broccoli

Servings: 6

Ingredients:

- 300g broccoli
- 300g cauliflower
- 2 tbsp oil
- ½ tsp garlic powder
- ¼ tsp salt
- ¼ tsp paprika
- ⅛ tsp pepper

Directions:

1. Preheat air fryer to 200°C
2. Place broccoli and cauliflower in a bowl and microwave for 3 minutes
3. Add remaining ingredients and mix well
4. Add to the air fryer and cook for about 12 mins

Lentil Burgers

Servings: 4

Ingredients:

- 100g black buluga lentils
- 1 carrot, grated
- 1 diced onion
- 100g white cabbage
- 300g oats
- 1 tbsp garlic puree
- 1 tsp cumin
- Salt and pepper

Directions:

1. Blend the oats until they resemble flour
2. Put the lentils in a pan with water and cook for 45 minutes
3. Steam your vegetables for 5 minutes
4. Add all the ingredients into a bowl and mix well to combine
5. Form into burgers place in the air fryer and cook at 180°C for 30 minutes

Potato Gratin

Servings: 4

Ingredients:

- 2 large potatoes
- 2 beaten eggs
- 100ml coconut cream
- 1 tbsp plain flour
- 50g grated cheddar

Directions:

1. Slice the potatoes into thin slices, place in the air fryer and cook for 10 minutes at 180°C
2. Mix eggs, coconut cream and flour together
3. Line four ramekins with the potato slices
4. Cover with the cream mixture, sprinkle with cheese and cook for 10 minutes at 200°C

Pakoras

Servings: 8

Ingredients:

- 200g chopped cauliflower
- 100g diced pepper
- 250g chickpea flour
- 30ml water
- ½ tsp cumin
- Cooking spray
- 1 onion, diced
- 1 tsp salt
- 1 garlic clove, minced
- 1 tsp curry powder
- 1 tsp coriander
- ½ tsp cayenne

Directions:

1. Preheat air fryer to 175°C
2. Place all ingredients in a bowl and mix well
3. Spray cooking basket with oil
4. Spoon 2 tbsp of mix into the basket and flatten, continue until the basket is full
5. Cook for 8 minutes, turn then cook for a further 8 minutes

Roasted Vegetable Pasta

Servings:4 | Cooking Time:15 Minutes

Ingredients:

- 400 g / 14 oz penne pasta
- 1 courgette, sliced
- 1 red pepper, deseeded and sliced
- 100 g / 3.5 oz mushroom, sliced
- 2 tbsp olive oil
- 1 tsp Italian seasoning
- 200 g cherry tomatoes, halved
- 2 tbsp fresh basil, chopped
- ½ tsp black pepper

Directions:

1. Cook the pasta according to the packet instructions.
2. Preheat the air fryer to 190 °C / 370 °F and line the air fryer with parchment paper or grease it with olive oil.
3. In a bowl, place the courgette, pepper, and mushroom, and toss in 2 tbsp olive oil
4. Place the vegetables in the air fryer and cook for 15 minutes.
5. Once the vegetables have softened, mix with the penne pasta, chopped cherry tomatoes, and fresh basil.
6. Serve while hot with a sprinkle of black pepper in each dish.

Mini Quiche

Servings: 2

Ingredients:

- 100g raw cashews
- 3 tbsp milk
- ½ tsp hot sauce
- 1 tsp white miso paste
- 1 tsp mustard
- 300g tofu
- 100g bacon pieces
- 1 chopped red pepper
- 1 chopped onion
- 6 tbsp yeast
- ½ tsp onion powder
- ½ tsp paprika
- ½ tsp cumin
- ½ tsp chilli powder
- ½ tsp black pepper
- ⅛ tsp turmeric
- ½ tsp canola oil
- 50g curly kale

Directions:

1. Heat the oil in a pan, add the bacon pepper, onion and curly kale and cook for about 3 minutes
2. Place all the other ingredients into a blender and blend until smooth
3. Add to a bowl with the bacon, pepper, onion and curly kale and mix well
4. Fill silicone muffin cups with the mix
5. Place in the air fryer and cook at 165ºC for 15 minutes

Courgette Meatballs

Servings: 4

Ingredients:

- 400g oats
- 40g feta, crumbled
- 1 beaten egg
- Salt and pepper
- 150g courgette
- 1 tsp lemon rind
- 6 basil leaves, thinly sliced
- 1 tsp dill
- 1 tsp oregano

Directions:

1. Preheat the air fryer to 200ºC
2. Grate the courgette into a bowl, squeeze any access water out
3. Add all the remaining ingredients apart from the oats and mix well
4. Blend the oats until they resemble breadcrumbs
5. Add the oats into the other mix and stir well
6. Form into balls and place in the air fryer cook for 10 minutes

Falafel Burgers

Servings: 2

Ingredients:

- 1 large can of chickpeas
- 1 onion
- 1 lemon
- 140g oats
- 28g grated cheese
- 28g feta cheese
- Salt and pepper to taste
- 3 tbsp Greek yogurt
- 4 tbsp soft cheese
- 1 tbsp garlic puree
- 1 tbsp coriander
- 1 tbsp oregano
- 1 tbsp parsley

Directions:

1. Place the chickpeas, onion, lemon rind, garlic and seasonings and blend until coarse
2. Add the mix to a bowl and stir in half the soft cheese, cheese and feta
3. Form in to burger shape and coat in the oats
4. Place in the air fryer and cook at 180ºC for 8 minutes
5. To make the sauce mix the remaining soft cheese, greek yogurt and lemon juice in a bowl

Bbq Sandwich

Servings: 2

Ingredients:

- 1 tbsp mayo
- ¼ tsp white wine vinegar
- ¼ tsp lemon juice
- 1/8 tsp garlic powder
- Pinch of salt
- Cabbage mix
- 2 sandwich buns
- 150g bbq soy curls

Directions:

1. Mix mayo, white wine vinegar, lemon juice, cabbage mix, garlic powder and pinch of salt to make coleslaw. Set aside
2. Add the buns to the air fryer and cook at 200ºC for 5 minutes to toast
3. Fill the buns with coleslaw, soy curls, pickles and chopped onions

Spicy Spanish Potatoes

Servings: 2

Ingredients:

- 4 large potatoes
- 1 tbsp olive oil
- 2 tsp paprika
- 2 tsp dried garlic
- 1 tsp barbacoa seasoning
- Salt and pepper

Directions:

1. Chop the potatoes into wedges
2. Place them in a bowl with olive oil and seasoning, mix well
3. Add to the air fryer and cook at 160°C for 20 minutes
4. Shake, increase heat to 200°C and cook for another 3 minutes

Tempura Veggies

Servings: 4

Ingredients:

- 150g flour
- ½ tsp salt
- ½ tsp pepper
- 2 eggs
- 2 tbsp cup water
- 100g avocado wedges
- 100g courgette slices
- 100g panko breadcrumbs
- 2 tsp oil
- 100g green beans
- 100g asparagus spears
- 100g red onion rings
- 100g pepper rings

Directions:

1. Mix together flour, salt and pepper. In another bowl mix eggs and water
2. Stir together panko crumbs and oil in a separate bowl
3. Dip vegetables in the flour mix, then egg and then the bread crumbs
4. Preheat the air fryer to 200°C
5. Place in the air fryer and cook for about 10 minutes until golden brown

Gnocchi Caprese

Servings: 2

Ingredients:

- 1 packet of gnocchi
- 150g cherry tomatoes, cut into halves
- 2 tbsp olive oil
- 2 tbsp balsamic vinegar
- 3 pressed cloves of garlic
- 200g basil, chopped
- 200g mini mozzarella balls
- 150g grated Parmesan
- Salt and pepper for seasoning

Directions:

1. Preheat the air fryer to 220°C
2. Take a large bowl and add the cherry tomatoes, gnocchi, oil, balsamic vinegar, garlic and seasoning, making sure that everything is well coated
3. Transfer to the air fryer basket
4. Cook for 10 minutes, shaking the basket every few minutes
5. Once cooked, transfer everything to a large mixing bowl and add the Parmesan cheese, coating well
6. Then, add the mozzarella and basil and toss once more

Aubergine Parmigiana

Servings: 2 As A Main Or 4 As A Side

Ingredients:

- 2 small or 1 large aubergine/eggplant, sliced 5 mm/¼ in. thick
- 1 tablespoon olive oil
- ¾ teaspoon salt
- 200 g/7 oz. mozzarella, sliced
- ½ teaspoon freshly ground black pepper
- 20 g/¼ cup finely grated Parmesan
- green vegetables, to serve
- SAUCE
- 135 g/5 oz. passata/strained tomatoes
- 1 teaspoon dried oregano
- ¼ teaspoon garlic salt
- 1 tablespoon olive oil

Directions:

1. Preheat the air-fryer to 200°C/400°F.
2. Rub each of the aubergine/eggplant slices with olive oil and salt. Divide the slices into two batches. Place one batch of the aubergine slices in the preheated air-fryer and air-fry for 4 minutes on one side, then turn over and air-fry for 2 minutes on the other side. Lay these on the base of a gratin dish that fits into your air-fryer.
3. Air-fry the second batch of aubergine slices in the same way. Whilst they're cooking, mix together the sauce ingredients in a small bowl.
4. Spread the sauce over the aubergines in the gratin dish. Add a layer of the mozzarella slices, then season with pepper. Add a second layer of aubergine slices, then top with Parmesan.
5. Place the gratin dish in the air-fryer and air-fry for 6 minutes, until the mozzarella is melted and the top of the dish is golden brown. Serve immediately with green vegetables on the side.

Macaroni & Cheese Quiche

Servings: 4

Ingredients:

- 8 tbsp macaroni pasta
- 1 block of short crust pastry
- 2 tbsp Greek yogurt
- 2 eggs
- 150ml milk
- 1 tsp garlic puree
- 400g grated cheese

Directions:

1. Rub the inside of 4 ramekins with flour
2. Line the ramekins with the pastry
3. Mix the yogurt, garlic and macaroni. Add to the ramekins until ¾ full
4. Mix the egg and milk together and pour over the macaroni. Sprinkle with cheese
5. Heat the air fryer to 180°C and cook for 20 minutes until golden brown.

Bagel Pizza

Servings: 1

Ingredients:

- 1 bagel
- 2 tbsp marinara sauce
- 6 slices vegan pepperoni
- 2 tbsp mozzarella
- Pinch of basil

Directions:

1. Heat the air fryer to 180°C
2. Cut the bagel in half and toast for 2 minutes in the air fryer
3. Remove from the air fryer and top with marinara sauce, pepperoni and mozzarella
4. Return to the air fryer and cook for 4-5 minutes
5. Sprinkle with basil to serve

Quinoa-stuffed Romano Peppers

Servings: 2

Ingredients:

- 1 tablespoon olive oil
- 1 onion, diced
- 1 garlic clove, chopped
- 100 g/⅔ cup uncooked quinoa
- 1½ tablespoons fajita seasoning
- 140 g/1 cup canned sweetcorn/corn kernels (drained weight)
- 3 romano peppers, sliced lengthways, seeds removed but stalk left intact
- 60 g/⅔ cup grated mature Cheddar

Directions:

1. Heat the oil in a saucepan. Add the onion and garlic and sauté for 5 minutes, until soft. Add the quinoa, fajita seasoning and 250 ml/1 cup water. Bring to a simmer, then cover with a lid and simmer for 15 minutes or until the quinoa is cooked and the water absorbed. Stir in the sweetcorn/corn kernels. Stuff each pepper half with the quinoa mixture, then top with grated cheese.
2. Preheat the air-fryer to 180°C/350°F.
3. Place the peppers on an air-fryer liner or a piece of pierced parchment paper, place in the preheated air-fryer and air-fry for 12–14 minutes, depending how 'chargrilled' you like your peppers.

Roasted Garlic

Servings: 2

Ingredients:

- 1 head of garlic
- Drizzle of olive oil
- Salt and pepper for seasoning

Directions:

1. Remove paper peel from garlic
2. Place in foil and drizzle with oil
3. Place in the air fryer and cook at 200°C for 20 minutes
4. Season before serving

Side Dishes Recipes

Side Dishes Recipes

Courgette Gratin

Servings: 2

Ingredients:

- 2 courgette
- 1 tbsp chopped parsley
- 2 tbsp breadcrumbs
- 4 tbsp grated parmesan
- 1 tbsp vegetable oil
- Salt and pepper to taste

Directions:

1. Heat the air fryer to 180°C
2. Cut each courgette in half length ways then slice
3. Mix the remaining ingredients together
4. Place the courgette in the air fryer and top with the breadcrumb mix
5. Cook for about 15 minutes until golden brown

Stuffing Filled Pumpkin

Servings: 2

Ingredients:

- 1/2 small pumpkin
- 1 diced parsnip
- 1 sweet potato, diced
- 1 diced onion
- 2 tsp dried mixed herbs
- 50g peas
- 1 carrot, diced
- 1 egg
- 2 minced garlic cloves

Directions:

1. Remove the seeds from the pumpkin
2. Combine all the other ingredients in a bowl
3. Stuff the pumpkin
4. Preheat the air fryer to 175°C
5. Place the pumpkin in the air fryer and cook for about 30 minutes

Super Easy Fries

Servings: 2

Ingredients:

- 500g potatoes cut into ½ inch sticks
- 1 tsp olive oil
- ¼ tsp salt
- ¼ tsp pepper

Directions:

1. Place the potatoes in a bowl cover with water and allow to soak for 30 minutes
2. Spread the butter onto one side of the bread slices
3. Pat dry with paper, drizzle with oil and toss to coat
4. Place in the air fryer and cook at 200°C for about 15 minutes, keep tossing through cooking time
5. Sprinkle with salt and pepper

Mediterranean Vegetables

Servings: 1–2

Ingredients:

- 1 courgette/zucchini, thickly sliced
- 1 (bell) pepper, deseeded and chopped into large chunks
- 1 red onion, sliced into wedges
- 12 cherry tomatoes
- 1 tablespoon olive oil
- ½ teaspoon salt
- ½ teaspoon freshly ground black pepper
- 2 rosemary twigs
- mozzarella, fresh pesto (see page 80) and basil leaves, to serve

Directions:

1. Preheat the air-fryer to 180°C/350°F.
2. Toss the prepared vegetables in the oil and seasoning. Add the vegetables and the rosemary to the preheated air-fryer and air-fry for 12–14 minutes, depending on how 'chargrilled' you like them.
3. Remove and serve topped with fresh mozzarella and pesto and scattered with basil leaves.

Ranch-style Potatoes

Servings: 2

Ingredients:

- 300g baby potatoes, washed
- 1 tbsp olive oil
- 3 tbsp dry ranch seasoning

Directions:

1. Preheat the air fryer to 220°C
2. Cut the potatoes in half
3. Take a mixing bowl and combine the olive oil with the ranch seasoning
4. Add the potatoes to the bowl and toss to coat
5. Cook for 15 minutes, shaking halfway through

Butternut Squash

Servings: 4

Ingredients:

- 500 g/1 lb. 2 oz. butternut squash, chopped into 2.5-cm/1-in. cubes
- 1 tablespoon olive oil or avocado oil
- 1 teaspoon smoked paprika
- 1 teaspoon dried oregano
- ½ teaspoon salt
- ¼ teaspoon freshly ground black pepper

Directions:

1. Preheat the air-fryer to 180ºC/350ºF.
2. In a bowl toss the butternut squash cubes in the oil and all the seasonings.
3. Add the butternut squash cubes to the preheated air-fryer and air-fry for 16–18 minutes, shaking the drawer once during cooking.

Bbq Beetroot Crisps

Servings:4 | Cooking Time:5 Minutes

Ingredients:

- 400 g / 14 oz beetroot, sliced
- 2 tbsp olive oil
- 1 tbsp BBQ seasoning
- ½ tsp black pepper

Directions:

1. Preheat the air fryer to 180 °C / 350 °F and line the bottom of the basket with parchment paper.
2. Place the beetroot slices in a large bowl. Add the olive oil, BBQ seasoning, and black pepper, and toss to coat the beetroot slices on both sides.
3. Place the beetroot slices in the air fryer and cook for 5 minutes until hot and crispy.

Tex Mex Hash Browns

Servings: 4

Ingredients:

- 500g potatoes cut into cubes
- 1 tbsp olive oil
- 1 red pepper
- 1 onion
- 1 jalapeño pepper
- ½ tsp taco seasoning
- ½ tsp cumin
- Salt and pepper to taste

Directions:

1. Soak the potatoes in water for 20 minutes
2. Heat the air fryer to 160ºC
3. Drain the potatoes and coat with olive oil
4. Add to the air fryer and cook for 18 minutes
5. Mix the remaining ingredients in a bowl, add the potatoes and mix well
6. Place the mix into the air fryer cook for 6 minutes, shake and cook for a further 5 minutes

Mexican Rice

Servings: 4

Ingredients:

- 500g long grain rice
- 3 tbsp olive oil
- 60ml water
- 1 tsp chilli powder
- 1/4 tsp cumin
- 2 tbsp tomato paste
- 1/2 tsp garlic powder
- 1tsp red pepper flakes
- 1 chopped onion
- 500ml chicken stock
- Half a small jalapeño pepper with seeds out, chopped
- Salt for seasoning

Directions:

1. Add the water and tomato paste and combine, placing to one side
2. Take a baking pan and add a little oil
3. Wash the rice and add to the baking pan
4. Add the chicken stock, tomato paste, jalapeños, onions, and the rest of the olive oil, and combine
5. Place aluminium foil over the top and place in your air fryer
6. Cook at 220°C for 50 minutes
7. Keep checking the rice as it cooks, as the liquid should be absorbing

Roasted Brussels Sprouts

Servings: 3

Ingredients:

- 300 g/10½ oz. Brussels sprouts, trimmed and halved
- 1 tablespoon olive oil
- ½ teaspoon salt
- ¼ teaspoon freshly ground black pepper

Directions:

1. Preheat the air-fryer to 160°C/325°F.
2. Toss the Brussels sprout halves in the oil and the seasoning. Add these to the preheated air-fryer and air-fry for 15 minutes, then increase the temperature of the air-fryer to 180°C/350°F and cook for a further 5 minutes until the sprouts are really crispy on the outside and cooked through.

Cheesy Broccoli

Servings:4 | Cooking Time:5 Minutes

Ingredients:

- 1 large broccoli head, broken into florets
- 4 tbsp soft cheese
- 1 tsp black pepper
- 50 g / 3.5 oz cheddar cheese, grated

Directions:

1. Preheat the air fryer to 150 °C / 300 °F and line the mesh basket with parchment paper or grease it with olive oil.
2. Wash and drain the broccoli florets and place in a bowl and stir in the soft cheese and black pepper to fully coat all of the florets.
3. Transfer the broccoli to the air fryer basket and sprinkle the cheddar cheese on top. Close the lid and cook for 5-7 minutes until the broccoli has softened and the cheese has melted.
4. Serve as a side dish to your favourite meal.

Zingy Roasted Carrots

Servings: 4

Ingredients:

- 500g carrots
- 1 tsp olive oil
- 1 tsp cayenne pepper
- Salt and pepper for seasoning

Directions:

1. Peel the carrots and cut them into chunks, around 2" in size
2. Preheat your air fryer to 220ºC
3. Add the carrots to a bowl with the olive oil and cayenne and toss to coat
4. Place in the fryer and cook for 15 minutes, giving them a stir halfway through
5. Season before serving

Homemade Croquettes

Servings:4 | Cooking Time:15 Minutes

Ingredients:

- 400 g / 14 oz white rice, uncooked
- 1 onion, sliced
- 2 cloves garlic, finely sliced
- 2 eggs, beaten
- 50 g / 3.5 oz parmesan cheese, grated
- 1 tsp salt
- 1 tsp black pepper
- 50 g / 3.5 oz breadcrumbs
- 1 tsp dried oregano

Directions:

1. In a large mixing bowl, combine the white rice, onion slices, garlic cloves slices, one beaten egg, parmesan cheese, and a sprinkle of salt and pepper.
2. Whisk the second egg in a separate bowl and place the breadcrumbs into another bowl.
3. Shape the mixture into 12 even croquettes and roll evenly in the egg, followed by the breadcrumbs.
4. Preheat the air fryer to 190 °C / 375 °F and line the bottom of the basket with parchment paper.
5. Place the croquettes in the lined air fryer basket and cook for 15 minutes, turning halfway through, until crispy and golden. Enjoy while hot as a side to your main dish.

Cheesy Garlic Asparagus

Servings: 4

Ingredients:

- 1 tsp olive oil
- 500g asparagus
- 1 tsp garlic salt
- 1 tbsp grated parmesan cheese
- Salt and pepper for seasoning

Directions:

1. Preheat the air fryer to 270ºC
2. Clean the asparagus and cut off the bottom 1"
3. Pat dry and place in the air fryer, covering with the oil
4. Sprinkle the parmesan and garlic salt on top, seasoning to your liking
5. Cook for between 7 and 10 minutes
6. Add a little extra parmesan over the top before serving

Sweet Potato Wedges

Servings:4 | Cooking Time:20 Minutes

Ingredients:

- ½ tsp garlic powder
- ½ tsp cumin
- ½ tsp smoked paprika
- ½ tsp cayenne pepper
- ½ tsp salt
- ½ tsp black pepper
- 1 tsp dried chives
- 4 tbsp olive oil
- 3 large sweet potatoes, cut into wedges

Directions:

1. Preheat the air fryer to 180 °C / 350 °F and line the bottom of the basket with parchment paper.
2. In a bowl, mix the garlic powder, cumin, smoked paprika, cayenne pepper, salt, black pepper, and dried chives until combined.
3. Whisk in the olive oil and coat the sweet potato wedges in the spicy oil mixture.
4. Transfer the coated sweet potatoes to the air fryer and close the lid. Cook for 20 minutes until cooked and crispy. Serve hot as a side with your main meal.

Sweet And Sticky Parsnips And Carrots

Servings:2 | Cooking Time:15 Minutes

Ingredients:

- 4 large carrots, peeled and chopped into long chunks
- 4 large parsnips, peeled and chopped into long chunks
- 1 tbsp olive oil
- 2 tbsp honey
- 1 tsp dried mixed herbs

Directions:

1. Preheat the air fryer to 150 °C / 300 °F and line the bottom of the basket with parchment paper.
2. Place the chopped carrots and parsnips in a large bowl and drizzle over the olive oil and honey. Sprinkle in some black pepper to taste and toss well to fully coat the vegetables.
3. Transfer the coated vegetables into the air fryer basket and shut the lid. Cook for 20 minutes until the carrots and parsnips and cooked and crispy.
4. Serve as a side with your dinner.

Asparagus Fries

Servings: 2

Ingredients:

- 1 egg
- 1 tsp honey
- 100g panko bread crumbs
- Pinch of cayenne pepper
- 100g grated parmesan
- 12 asparagus spears
- 75g mustard
- 75g Greek yogurt

Directions:

1. Preheat air fryer to 200°C
2. Combine egg and honey in a bowl, mix panko crumbs and parmesan on a plate
3. Coat each asparagus in egg then in the bread crumbs
4. Place in the air fryer and cook for about 6 mins
5. Mix the remaining ingredients in a bowl and serve as a dipping sauce

Spicy Green Beans

Servings: 4

Ingredients:

- 300g green beans
- 1 tbsp sesame oil
- 1 tsp soy
- 1 tsp rice wine vinegar
- 1 clove garlic, minced
- 1 tsp red pepper flakes

Directions:

1. Preheat air fryer to 200°C
2. Place green beans in a bowl
3. Mix together remaining ingredients, add green beans and fully coat
4. Place in the air fryer and cook for 12 minutes

Honey Roasted Parsnips

Servings: 4

Ingredients:

- 350 g/12 oz. parsnips
- 1 tablespoon plain/all-purpose flour (gluten-free if you wish)
- 1½ tablespoons runny honey
- 2 tablespoons olive oil
- salt

Directions:

1. Top and tail the parsnips, then slice lengthways, about 2 cm/¾ in. wide. Place in a saucepan with water to cover and a good pinch of salt. Bring to the boil, then boil for 5 minutes.
2. Remove and drain well, allowing any excess water to evaporate. Dust the parsnips with flour. Mix together the honey and oil in a small bowl, then toss in the parsnips to coat well in the honey and oil.
3. Preheat the air-fryer to 180°C/350°F.
4. Add the parsnips to the preheated air-fryer and air-fry for 14–16 minutes, depending on how dark you like the outsides (the longer you cook them, the sweeter they get).

Whole Sweet Potatoes

Servings: 4 As A Side Or Snack

Ingredients:

- 4 medium sweet potatoes
- 1 tablespoon olive oil
- 1 teaspoon salt
- toppings of your choice

Directions:

1. Preheat the air-fryer to 200°C/400°F.
2. Wash and remove any imperfections from the skin of the sweet potatoes, then rub the potatoes with the olive oil and salt.
3. Add the sweet potatoes to the preheated air-fryer and air-fry for up to 40 minutes (the cooking time depends on the size of the potatoes). Remove as soon as they are soft when pierced. Slice open and serve with your choice of toppings.
4. VARIATION: WHOLE JACKET POTATOES
5. Regular baking potatoes can be air-fried in the same way, but will require a cooking time of 45–60 minutes, depending on their size.

Carrot & Parmesan Chips

Servings: 2

Ingredients:

- 180g carrots
- 1 tbsp olive oil
- 2 tbsp grated parmesan
- 1 crushed garlic clove
- Salt and pepper for seasoning

Directions:

1. Take a mixing bowl and add the olive oil and garlic, combining well
2. Remove the tops of the carrots and cut into halves, and then another half
3. Add the carrots to the bowl and toss well
4. Add the parmesan and coat the carrots well
5. Add the carrots to the air fryer and cook for 20 minutes at 220ºC, shaking halfway through

Onion Rings

Servings: 4

Ingredients:

- 200g flour
- 75g cornstarch
- 2 tsp baking powder
- 1 tsp salt
- 2 pinches of paprika
- 1 large onion, cut into rings
- 1 egg
- 1 cup milk
- 200g breadcrumbs
- 2 pinches garlic powder

Directions:

1. Stir flour, salt, starch and baking powder together in a bowl
2. Dip onion rings into the flour mix to coat
3. Whisk the egg and milk into the flour mix, dip in the onion rings
4. Dip the onion rings into the bread crumbs
5. Heat the air fryer to 200ºC
6. Place the onion rings in the air fryer and cook for 2-3 minutes until golden brown
7. Sprinkle with paprika and garlic powder to serve

Desserts Recipes

Desserts Recipes

Mini Egg Buns

Servings: 8

Ingredients:

- 100g self raising flour
- 100g caster sugar
- 100g butter
- 2 eggs
- 2 tbsp honey
- 1 tbsp vanilla essence
- 300g soft cheese
- 100g icing sugar
- 2 packets of Mini Eggs

Directions:

1. Cream the butter and sugar together until light and fluffy, beat in the eggs one at a time
2. Add the honey and vanilla essence, fold in the flour a bit at a time
3. Divide the mix into 8 bun cases and place in the air fryer. Cook at 180°C for about 20 minutes
4. Cream the soft cheese and icing sugar together to make the topping
5. Allow the buns to cool, pipe on the topping mix and add mini eggs

Cinnamon Bites

Servings: 8

Ingredients:

- 200g flour
- 200g whole wheat flour
- 2 tbsp sugar
- 1 tsp baking powder
- ¼ tsp cinnamon
- 3 tbsp water
- ¼ tsp salt
- 4 tbsp butter
- 25ml milk
- Cooking spray
- 350g powdered sugar

Directions:

1. Mix together flour, sugar, baking powder and salt in a bowl
2. Add the butter and mix well
3. Add the milk and mix to form a dough
4. Knead until dough is smooth, cut into 16 pieces
5. Roll each piece into a small ball
6. Coat the air fryer with cooking spray and heat to 175°C
7. Add the balls to the air fryer and cook for 12 minutes
8. Mix the powdered sugar and water together, decorate

Banana Cake

Servings: 4

Ingredients:

- Cooking spray
- 25g brown sugar
- ½ tbsp butter
- 1 banana, mashed
- 1 egg
- 2 tbsp honey
- 225g self raising flour
- ½ tsp cinnamon
- Pinch salt

Directions:

1. Preheat air fryer to 160ºC
2. Spray a small fluted tube tray with cooking spray
3. Beat sugar and butter together in a bowl until creamy
4. Combine the banana egg and honey together in another bowl
5. Mix into the butter until smooth
6. Sift in the remaining ingredients and mix well
7. Spoon into the tray and cook in the air fryer for 30 minutes

Fruit Crumble

Servings: 2

Ingredients:

- 1 diced apple
- 75g frozen blackberries
- 25g brown rice flour
- 2 tbsp sugar
- ½ tsp cinnamon
- 2 tbsp butter

Directions:

1. Preheat air fryer to 150ºC
2. Mix apple and blackberries in an air fryer safe baking pan
3. In a bowl mix the flour, sugar, cinnamon and butter, spoon over the fruit
4. Cook for 15 minutes

Chonut Holes

Servings: 12

Ingredients:

- 225g flour
- 75g sugar
- 1 tsp baking powder
- ¼ tsp cinnamon
- 2 tbsp sugar
- ½ tsp salt
- 2 tbsp aquafaba
- 1 tbsp melted coconut oil
- 75ml soy milk
- 2 tsp cinnamon

Directions:

1. In a bowl mix the flour, ¼ cup sugar, baking powder, ¼ tsp cinnamon and salt
2. Add the aquafaba, coconut oil and soy milk mix well
3. In another bowl mix 2 tsp cinnamon and 2 tbsp sugar
4. Line the air fryer with parchment paper
5. Divide the dough into 12 pieces and dredge with the cinnamon sugar mix
6. Place in the air fryer at 185°C and cook for 6-8 minutes, don't shake them

Fried Oreos

Servings: 8

Ingredients:

- 1 tube crescent rolls
- 8 Oreos

Directions:

1. Wrap the Oreos in the crescent roll dough, trim off any excess
2. Spray the air fryer with cooking spray
3. Place Oreos in the air fryer and cook at 175°C for 6 minutes

Banana Bread

Servings: 8

Ingredients:

- 200g flour
- 1 tsp cinnamon
- ½ tsp salt
- ¼ tsp baking soda
- 2 ripe banana mashed
- 2 large eggs
- 75g sugar
- 25g plain yogurt
- 2 tbsp oil
- 1 tsp vanilla extract
- 2 tbsp chopped walnuts
- Cooking spray

Directions:

1. Line a 6 inch cake tin with parchment paper and coat with cooking spray
2. Whisk together flour, cinnamon, salt and baking soda set aside
3. In another bowl mix together remaining ingredients, add the flour mix and combine well
4. Pour batter into the cake tin and place in the air fryer
5. Cook at 155°C for 35 minutes turning halfway through

S'mores

Servings: 2

Ingredients:

- 2 graham crackers, broken in half
- 2 marshmallows, halved
- 2 pieces of chocolate

Directions:

1. Place 2 halves of graham crackers in the air fryer and add a marshmallow to each sticky side down
2. Cook in the air fryer at 180°C for 5 minutes until the marshmallows are golden
3. Remove from the air fryer add a piece of chocolate and top with the other half of graham crackers

New York Cheesecake

Servings: 8

Ingredients:

- 225g plain flour
- 100g brown sugar
- 100g butter
- 50g melted butter
- 1 tbsp vanilla essence
- 750g soft cheese
- 2 cups caster sugar
- 3 large eggs
- 50ml quark

Directions:

1. Add the flour, sugar, and 100g butter to a bowl and mix until combined. Form into biscuit shapes place in the air fryer and cook for 15 minutes at 180°C
2. Grease a springform tin
3. Break the biscuits up and mix with the melted butter, press firmly into the tin
4. Mix the soft cheese and sugar in a bowl until creamy, add the eggs and vanilla and mix. Mix in the quark
5. Pour the cheesecake batter into the pan
6. Place in your air fryer and cook for 30 minutes at 180°C. Leave in the air fryer for 30 minutes whilst it cools
7. Refrigerate for 6 hours

Cinnamon Biscuit Bites

Servings: 16

Ingredients:
- 200g flour
- 200g wholewheat flour
- 2 tbsp sugar
- 1 tsp baking powder
- ¼ tsp cinnamon
- ¼ tsp salt
- 4 tbsp butter
- 50ml milk
- Cooking spray
- 300g icing sugar
- 3 tbsp water

Directions:

1. Mix together flour, salt, sugar baking powder and cinnamon in a bowl
2. Add butter and mix until well combined
3. Add milk and form a dough, place dough on a floured surface and knead until smooth
4. Cut into 16 equal pieces and form each piece into a ball
5. Place in the air fryer and cook at 180ºC for about 12 minutes
6. Mix together icing sugar and water and coat to serve

Peanut Butter And Banana Bites

Servings: 12

Ingredients:
- 1 banana
- 12 wonton wrappers
- 75g peanut butter
- 1-2 tsp vegetable oil

Directions:

1. Slice the banana and place in a bowl of water with lemon juice to prevent browning
2. Place one piece of banana and a spoon of peanut butter in each wonton wrapper
3. Wet the edges of each wrapper and fold over to seal
4. Spray the air fryer with oil
5. Place in the air fryer and cook at 190ºC for 6 minutes

Strawberry Lemonade Pop Tarts

Servings: 12

Ingredients:

- 300g whole wheat flour
- 225g white flour
- ¼ tsp salt
- 2 tbsp light brown sugar
- 300g icing sugar
- 2 tbsp lemon juice
- Zest of 1 lemon
- 150g cold coconut oil
- 1 tsp vanilla extract
- 75ml ice cold water
- Strawberry Jam
- 1 tsp melted coconut oil
- ¼ tsp vanilla extract
- Sprinkles

Directions:

1. In a bowl mix the flours, salt and sugar. Mix in the cold coconut oil
2. Add 1 tsp vanilla and 1 tbsp at a time of the ice cold water, mix until a dough is formed
3. Take the dough and roll out thinly on a floured surface. Cut into 5cm by 7cm rectangles
4. Place a tsp of jam in the centre of half the rectangles, wet the edges place another rectangle on the top and seal
5. Place in the air fryer and cook at 200ºC for 10 minutes. Allow to cool
6. Mix the icing sugar, coconut oil, lemon juice and lemon zest in a bowl. Mix well. Top the pop tarts and add sprinkles to serve

Peach Pies

Servings: 8

Ingredients:

- 2 peaches, peeled and chopped
- 1 tbsp lemon juice
- 3 tbsp sugar
- 1 tsp vanilla extract
- ¼ tsp salt
- 1 tsp cornstarch
- 1 pack of shortcrust pastry

Directions:

1. Stir together peaches, lemon juice, sugar, vanilla and salt allow to stand for 15 minutes
2. Drain the peaches keeping 1 tbsp of the juice
3. Mix the liquid with the cornstarch and mix into the peaches
4. Cut out 8 4 inch circles from the pastry. Add 1 tbsp of peach mix to each piece of pastry
5. Fold the dough over to create half moons, crimp the edges with a fork to seal. Spray with cooking spray
6. Place in the air fryer and cook at 180ºC for 12-14 minutes

French Toast Sticks

Servings: 12

Ingredients:

- 2 eggs
- 25g milk
- 1 tbsp melted butter
- 1 tsp vanilla extract
- 1 tsp cinnamon
- 4 slices bread, cut into thirds
- 1 tsp icing sugar

Directions:

1. Mix eggs, milk, butter, vanilla and cinnamon together in a bowl
2. Line the air fryer with parchment paper
3. Dip each piece of bread into the egg mixture
4. Place in the air fryer and cook at 190ºC for 6 minutes, turn over and cook for another 3 minutes
5. Sprinkle with icing sugar to serve

Lava Cakes

Servings: 4

Ingredients:

- 1 ½ tbsp self raising flour
- 3 ½ tbsp sugar
- 150g butter
- 150g dark chocolate, chopped
- 2 eggs

Directions:

1. Preheat the air fryer to 175ºC
2. Grease 4 ramekin dishes
3. Melt chocolate and butter in the microwave for about 3 minutes
4. Whisk the eggs and sugar together until pale and frothy
5. Pour melted chocolate into the eggs and stir in the flour
6. Fill the ramekins ¾ full, place in the air fryer and cook for 10 minutes

Banana Maple Flapjack

Servings:9

Ingredients:

- 100 g/7 tablespoons butter (or plant-based spread if you wish)
- 75 g/5 tablespoons maple syrup
- 2 ripe bananas, mashed well with the back of a fork
- 1 teaspoon vanilla extract
- 240 g/2½ cups rolled oats/quick-cooking oats

Directions:

1. Gently heat the butter and maple syrup in a medium saucepan over a low heat until melted. Stir in the mashed banana, vanilla and oats and combine all ingredients. Pour the flapjack mixture into a 15 x 15-cm/6 x 6-in. baking pan and cover with foil.
2. Preheat the air-fryer to 200ºC/400ºF.
3. Add the baking pan to the preheated air-fryer and air-fry for 12 minutes, then remove the foil and cook for a further 4 minutes to brown the top. Leave to cool before cutting into 9 squares.

Birthday Cheesecake

Servings: 8

Ingredients:
- 6 Digestive biscuits
- 50g melted butter
- 800g soft cheese
- 500g caster sugar
- 4 tbsp cocoa powder
- 6 eggs
- 2 tbsp honey
- 1 tbsp vanilla

Directions:

1. Flour a spring form tin to prevent sticking
2. Crush the biscuits and then mix with the melted butter, press into the bottom and sides of the tin
3. Mix the caster sugar and soft cheese with an electric mixer. Add 5 eggs, honey and vanilla. Mix well
4. Spoon half the mix into the pan and pat down well. Place in the air fryer and cook at 180°C for 20 minutes then 160°C for 15 minutes and then 150°C for 20 minutes
5. Mix the cocoa and the last egg into the remaining mix. Spoon over the over the bottom layer and place in the fridge. Chill for 11 hours

Pumpkin Spiced Bread Pudding

Servings: 2

Ingredients:
- 175g heavy cream
- 500g pumpkin puree
- 30ml milk
- 25g sugar
- 1 large egg, plus one extra yolk
- ⅛ tsp salt
- ½ tsp pumpkin spice
- 500g cubed crusty bread
- 4 tbsp butter

Directions:

1. Place all of the ingredients apart from the bread and butter into a bowl and mix.
2. Add the bread and melted butter to the bowl and mix well
3. Heat the air fryer to 175°C
4. Pour the mix into a baking tin and cook in the air fryer for 35-40 minutes
5. Serve with maple cream

Breakfast Muffins

Servings:4

Ingredients:

- 1 eating apple, cored and grated
- 40 g/2 heaped tablespoons maple syrup
- 40 ml/3 tablespoons oil (avocado, olive or coconut), plus extra for greasing
- 1 egg
- 40 ml/3 tablespoons milk (plant-based if you wish)
- 90 g/scant ¾ cup brown rice flour
- 50 g/½ cup ground almonds
- ¾ teaspoon ground cinnamon
- ⅛ teaspoon ground cloves
- ¼ teaspoon salt
- 1 teaspoon baking powder
- Greek or plant-based yogurt and fresh fruit, to serve

Directions:

1. In a bowl mix the grated apple, maple syrup, oil, egg and milk. In another bowl mix the rice flour, ground almonds, cinnamon, cloves, salt and baking powder. Combine the wet ingredients with the dry, mixing until there are no visible patches of the flour mixture left. Grease 4 ramekins and divide the batter equally between them.
2. Preheat the air-fryer to 160°C/325°F.
3. Add the ramekins to the preheated air-fryer and air-fry for 12 minutes. Check the muffins are cooked by inserting a cocktail stick/toothpick into the middle of one of the muffins. If it comes out clean, the muffins are ready; if not, cook for a further couple of minutes.
4. Allow to cool in the ramekins, then remove and serve with your choice of yogurt and fresh fruit.

Chocolate Dipped Biscuits

Servings: 6

Ingredients:

- 225g self raising flour
- 100g sugar
- 100g butter
- 50g milk chocolate
- 1 egg beaten
- 1 tsp vanilla essence

Directions:

1. Add the flour, butter and sugar to a bowl and rub together
2. Add the egg and vanilla, mix to form a dough
3. Split the dough into 6 and form into balls
4. Place in the air fryer cook at 180°C for 15 minutes
5. Melt the chocolate, dip the cooked biscuits into the chocolate and half cover

Special Oreos

Servings: 9

Ingredients:

- 100g pancake mix
- 25ml water
- Cooking spray
- 9 Oreos
- 1 tbsp icing sugar

Directions:

1. Mix pancake mix and water until well combined
2. Line the air fryer with parchment paper and spray with cooking spray
3. Preheat the air fryer to 200°C
4. Dip each cookie in the pancake mix and place in the air fryer
5. Cook for 5 minutes, turn and cook for a further 3 minutes
6. Sprinkle with icing sugar to serve

Chocolate Eclairs

Servings: 9

Ingredients:

- 100g plain flour
- 50g butter
- 3 eggs
- 150ml water
- 25g butter
- 1 tsp vanilla extract
- 1 tsp icing sugar
- 150ml whipped cream
- 50g milk chocolate
- 1 tbsp whipped cream

Directions:

1. Preheat the air fryer to 180°C
2. Add 50g of butter to a pan along with the water and melt over a medium heat
3. Remove from the heat and stir in the flour. Return to the heat until mix form a single ball of dough
4. Allow to cool, once cool beat in the eggs until you have a smooth dough
5. Make into eclair shapes, cook in the air fryer at 180°C for 10 minutes and then 160°C for 8 minutes
6. Mix the vanilla, icing sugar and 150ml of whipping cream until nice and thick
7. Once cool fill each eclair with the cream mix
8. Place the chocolate, 1 tbsp whipped cream and 25g of butter in a glass bowl and melt over a pan of boiling water. Top the eclairs

Appendix : Recipes Index

E

F

G

H

T

V

W

Z

Printed in Great Britain
by Amazon